SONGS OF PRAISE

Combined Edition

EDITOR'S NOTE

The *Songs of Praise* series was designed to meet the need in churches and prayer groups for legal songbooks containing effective and popular worship music from many copyright sources. These songs were selected for their ability to draw groups together in the worship of God and the sharing of his word.

Now, for the convenience of those who are encountering *Songs of Praise* for the first time and of those groups who need to replace copies or add to their present collections, Servant Music presents the *Combined Edition*.

In order to make the *Combined Edition* easy to use alongside the original songbooks, we have retained the original numbering system and song order. The songs within each volume section are arranged alphabetically and numbered 1-79 for *Volume 1*, 201-241 for *Volume 2*, 301-339 for *Volume 3*, and 401-428 for *Volume 4*. A complete title and first line index is located at the back of the book to aid in locating any particular song.

ACKNOWLEDGEMENTS

We wish to thank World Library Publications, Inc., F.E.L. Publications, Ltd., Mills Music, Inc., and all others who have given permission for their songs to be included in *Songs of Praise: Combined Edition*. Any errors or omissions will be cheerfully corrected in future printings.

Most of the songs in this collection are copyrighted. Please remember that further reproduction of any kind without the express permission of the copyright owner is in violation of the law. Please refer to the notices underneath the songs for the names of the respective copyright owners.

The selections "All of My Life," "I Am the Resurrection," "Song of Thanks," and "They'll Know We Are Christians by Our Love" have been printed with permission of F.E.L. Publications, Ltd., 1925 Pontius Ave., Los Angeles, CA 90025. Phone (213) 478-0053. Further reproduction is not permitted without permission of the copyright owner.

Songs of Praise: Combined Edition and the four separate original volumes may be ordered from

Servant Publications
P.O. Box 8617
Ann Arbor, Michigan 48107
U.S.A.

Hardcover Edition: ISBN 0-89283-173-1
Paperback Edition: ISBN 0-89283-172-3

Illustrations by Peg Hosford

Compiled by **THE WORD OF GOD MUSIC**

Published by **SERVANT MUSIC**

Printed in the United States of America.

TABLE OF CONTENTS

All of Your People

Words and Music by
James Berlucchi

Verses may be sung either in E major or in E minor. While the verses printed here may be sung,
is it customary to improvise verses following the chord progression given. The verses printed
here are given as examples of what may be done.
The verses in E major are especially appropriate for large gatherings, while the verses in E
minor may work best for very small groups or for private singing.

VERSES IN E MAJOR

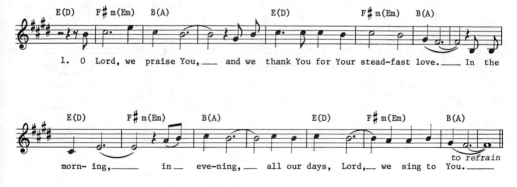

Continued ▶

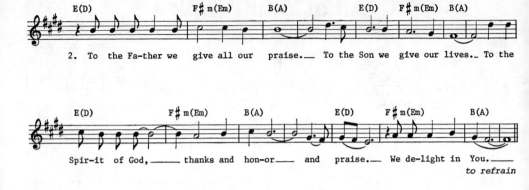

E(D)   F♯m(Em)   B(A)   E(D)   F♯m(Em)   B(A)

2. To the Fa-ther we give all our praise.__ To the Son we give our lives.__ To the

E(D)   F♯m(Em)   B(A)   E(D)   F♯m(Em)   B(A)

Spir-it of God,____ thanks and hon-or____ and praise.__ We de-light in You.____

to refrain

VERSES IN E MINOR

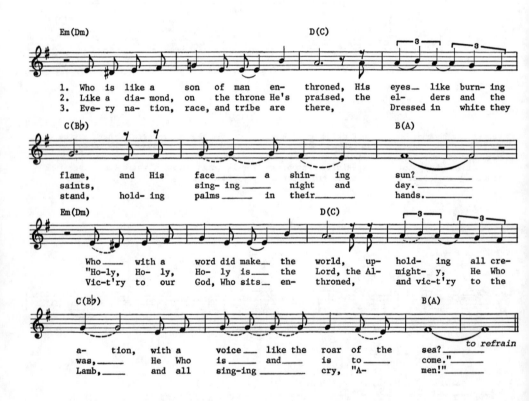

Em(Dm)   D(C)

1. Who is like a   son of man en-   throned, His eyes__ like burn-ing
2. Like a dia-mond, on the throne He's praised, the el-ders and the
3. Eve-ry na-tion, race, and tribe are there, Dressed in white they

C(B♭)   B(A)

flame,   and His   face_____ a shin-ing   sun?_____
saints,   sing-ing_____ night and day._____
stand,   hold-ing   palms_____ in their_____ hands._____

Em(Dm)   D(C)

Who____ with a   word did make__ the world, up-hold-ing all cre-
"Ho-ly, Ho-ly, Ho-ly is__ the Lord, the Al-might-y, He Who
Vic-t'ry to our God, Who sits__ en-throned, and vic-t'ry to the

C(B♭)   B(A)

a-   tion, with a   voice__ like the roar of the   sea?_____
was,____   He Who is____ and____ is to____ come."____
Lamb,____ and all sing-ing_____ cry, "A-men!"____

to refrain

Allelu!

MILDRED (Mimi) ARMSTRONG

Solo 1. Come and bless, come and praise, come and praise the liv-ing God.

CHORUS Al - le - lu, Al - le - lu, Al - le - lu - ia, Je-sus Christ.

All Al - le - lu, Al - le - lu, Al - le - lu - ia, Je-sus Christ.
Al - le - lu, Al - le - lu, Al - le - lu - ia, Je-sus Christ.

2. Come and seek, come and find, come and find the living God.
   Allelu, Allelu, Alleluia, Jesus Christ.

3. Come and hear, come and know, come and know the living God.
   Allelu, Allelu, Alleluia, Jesus Christ.

4. Come and bless, come and praise, come and praise the Word of God.
   Word of God, Word made flesh, Alleluia, Jesus, Christ.

5. Come behold, come and see, come and see the newborn babe.
   Allelu, Allelu, Alleluia, Jesus Christ.

6. Angel choirs sing above, "Glory to the Son of God!"
   Shepherd folk sing below, "Allelu, Emmanuel!"

7. Allelu, Allelu, Allelu, Emmanuel!
   Allelu, Allelu, Allelu, Emmanuel!

3

Alleluia

Words and Music by
Jerry Sinclair

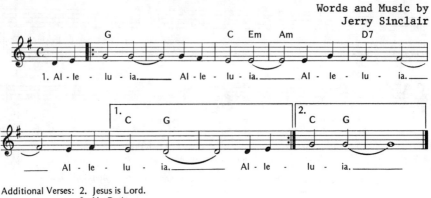

1. Al - le - lu - ia.___ Al - le - lu - ia.___ Al - le - lu - ia.___

1. ___ Al - le - lu - ia.___
2. Al - le - lu - ia.___

Additional Verses: 2. Jesus is Lord.
 3. My Redeemer.
 4. Come, Lord Jesus.

4

Alleluia No. 1

Words and Music by
Donald Fishel

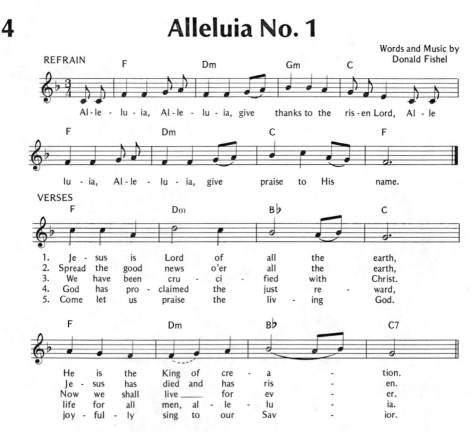

REFRAIN

Al - le - lu - ia, Al - le - lu - ia, give thanks to the ris - en Lord, Al - le

lu - ia, Al - le - lu - ia, give praise to His name.

VERSES

1. Je - sus is Lord of all the earth,
2. Spread the good news o'er all the earth,
3. We have been pro - cru - ci - fied with Christ.
4. God has pro - claimed the just re - ward,
5. Come let us praise the liv - ing God.

He is the King of cre - a - tion.
Je - sus has died and has ris - en.
Now we shall live___ for ev - er.
life for all men, al - le - lu - ia.
joy - ful - ly sing to our Sav - ior.

Alleluia, Sons of God Arise

5

6 The Angel of the Lord

Psalm 34:7-8

Unknown

The an- gel of the Lord___ en- camp-eth round a- bout them that fear him___

___ and de- liv-ers them.___ The ___ Oh, taste and see that the Lord is___ good.

Hap-py is the man that___ trust-eth in Him. Oh,___ taste and see that the

Lord is___ good. Hap- py is the man that trust-eth in Him.___

Away They Went With Weeping

7

Adapted from Psalm 126 by J.J.C.

James J. Cavnar

A- way they went with weep-ing, car- ry- ing the seed;
back, they came back sing- ing with their sheaves.

They who sow in tears shall reap with laugh- ter;
they who sow in tears shall sing.

1. When Yah- weh brought Zi- on's ___ cap- tives home, at
2. E- ven the pa- gans ___ start- ed talk- ing a-
3. From bond- age ___ Yah- weh, de- liv- er us ___ as

first it ___ seemed ___ like a dream. ___ Then our mouths ___
bout the mar- vels the ___ Lord had done. What ___ mar- vels
streams in a des-ert ___ land. ___ Those who went out

filled ___ with laugh-ter and our lips ___ with song. ___
He ___ did for us, and ___ how we were glad! ___
sow-ing in tears, ___ they shall sing as they reap. ___

G9

8

Balm in Gilead

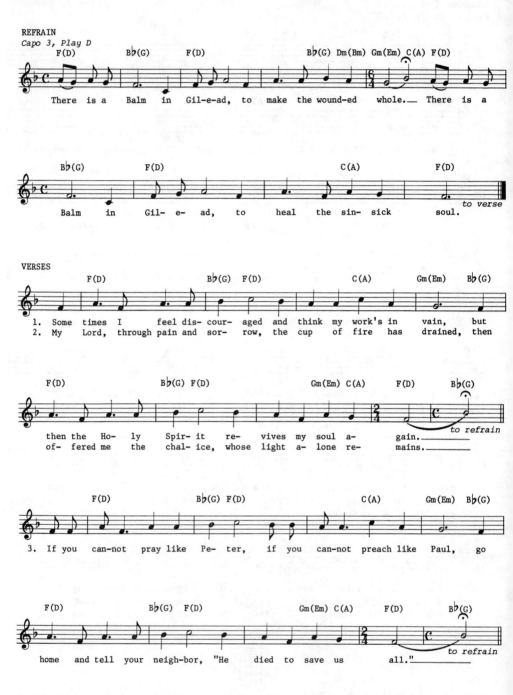

Bless the Lord, O My Soul

9

Psalm 103:1

Unknown

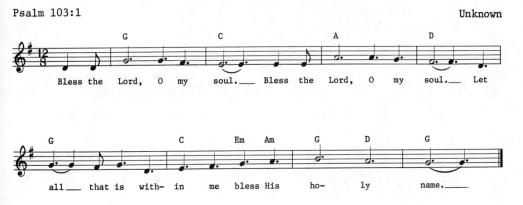

Bless the Lord, O my soul.___ Bless the Lord, O my soul.___ Let

all___ that is with- in me bless His ho- ly name.___

The Breath of God

10

Words and Music by
William E. Booth-Clibborn

Let it breathe on me, let it breathe on me. Let this

breath of God now breathe on me. Let it breathe on me, let it

breathe on me. Let this breath of God now breathe on me.

11 Canticle of the Gift

Text: Refrain by Pat Uhl
Verses by Michael Gilligan

Music by
Pat Uhl

REFRAIN

O what a gift, What a won-der-ful gift; Who can tell the won-ders of the Lord? Let us o-pen our eyes, our ears, and our hearts; it is Christ the Lord, it is He!

to verse

VERSES

1. In the still-ness of the night, when the world was a-sleep, the Lord made His mes-sage known. It was then that His Word came down from on high, from the Fa-ther's roy-al throne: Christ our Lord and our King!

to refrain

2. His mighty Word cuts quick and clean,
far sharper than a two-edged sword:
Open your eyes, your ears, and your hearts,
and hear the Word of the Lord:
Christ our Lord and our King!

3. He came to his people, the chosen race,
that his Father's will would be known;
Lion of Judah, Light of the World,
our Redeemer came to his own:
Christ our Lord and our King!

4. He lived here among us, he worked here among us,
   morning, night, and day;
   Showed us his glory, gave us a promise,
   and then we turned away:
   Christ our Lord and our King!

5. At the Passover meal on the night before he died,
   he lifted up his eyes and prayed
   Then he broke the bread, then he shared the wine--
   the gift that God had made:
   Christ our Lord and our King!

6. On the hill of Calvary, the world held its breath;
   and there for the world to see,
   the Father gave his Son, his very own Son
   for the love of you and me:
   Christ our Lord and our King!

7. Early on that morning when the guards were sleeping,
   the Father revealed his might;
   Christ in his glory arose from the dead,
   the Lord of Life and Light:
   Christ our Lord and our King!

8. On the road to Emmayus, the glory that is his,
   the disciples could never see.
   Then he broke the bread, then he shared the wine;
   it is the Lord, it is he:
   Christ our Lord and our King!

9. Now look around you and open your eyes;
   remember the Spirit is here.
   Here within his Church, his people are one.
   Look, the Lord is near:
   Christ our Lord and our King!

Canticle of the Three Young Men 12

Verses adapted from Daniel 3

Music and Refrain by
an anonymous Canadian

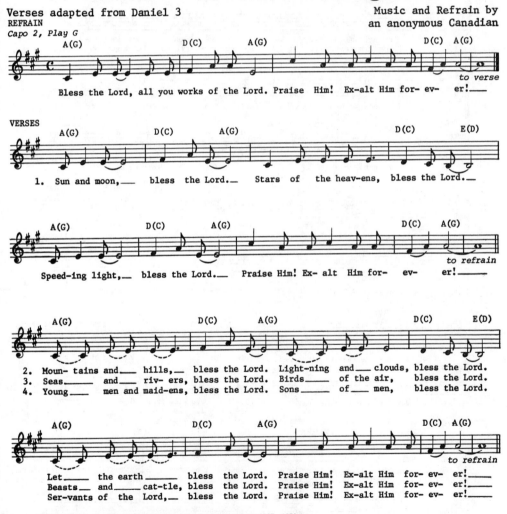

13 Come All Ye Nations

Words and Music by
Charles Christmas

Come, Follow Me

14

Words and Music by
Ann Cadwallader

15   Come, Go With Me to That Land

Unknown

Come, go with me to that land. Come, go with me to that land. Come, go
with me to that land where I'm bound.___ Come, go with me to that land. Come, go
with me to that land, to that land, to that land where I'm bound.___

Any of the following verses, or spontaneous verses, may also be used.

Be singing and dancing in that land . . .
There's milk and honey in that land . . .
You're gonna meet Jesus in that land . . .
Well, don't you know heaven is that land . . .

16   Come Holy Ghost

Veni Creator Spiritus
Rabanus Maurus, 776-856 (?)
Tr. Edward Caswall, 1849, alt.

Louis Lambillotte, S. J.

1. Come, Ho-ly Ghost, Cre-a-tor blest,
2. O Com-fort blest, to thee we cry,
3. Praise be to thee, Fa-ther and Son,

1. And in our hearts take up thy rest;
2. Thou heav'n-ly Gift of God most High;
3. And Ho-ly Spir-it, Three in One;

1. Come with thy grace and heav'n-ly aid
2. Thou Font of life, and Fire of love,
3. And may the Son on us be-stow

1. To fill the hearts which thou hast made. made.
2. And sweet A-noint-ing from a-bove. bove.
3. The gifts that from the Spir-it flow. flow.

Consider the Lilies

17

Matthew 6:25-34
Adapted by Jean Goeboro

Music by Jean Goeboro

REFRAIN

Con - si - der the lil - ies of __ the field; they nei - ther toil nor spin. __ Yet

I tell you that ev-en Sol - o - mon was not __ ar - rayed like these. these. __

to verse

1. What shall we eat, Lord? What shall we drink? What shall we put on to - day?
2. The birds of the air don't toil or reap, yet our good Fa - ther feeds them.
3. If God so clothes the grass of the field, which is a - live and then burned,
4. Do not be anx - ious for to - mor - row. Let each day's trou - ble suf - fice.

Is not life more than food, __ the bod - y more than clothes? __
Are you not of more worth __ in the eyes of God? __
will the Lord not much more __ give clothes to His chil - dren? __
Seek first His king - dom, __ and all things will be yours. __

18 The Dancing Heart

Words and Music by
Roy Turner

REFRAIN

Oh, the Ho-ly Ghost will set your feet a danc-ing,____ the Ho-ly Ghost will thrill you thru and thru;____ the Ho-ly Ghost will set your feet a danc-ing,____ and set your heart a danc-ing too.____

VERSES

1. Da- vid danced be- fore the Lord, he danced with all his might, His
2. Da- vid danced be- fore the Lord to mag- ni- fy His name; In
3. Out of E- gypt long a- go, the Is- rael- ites were led;
4. There was a cel- e- bra- tion____ up- on the Red Sea shore;
5. The prod-i- gal was far a- way,____ wan- d'ring out in sin, But
6. The fa- ther's house with mu- sic rang to wel- come home the son;
7. Now man- y saints are cold and bound by un- be- lief to- day, They
8. Now in the Bi- ble we can read that in the lat- ter days,

1. heart was filled with Ho- ly joy, his spir- it was so light;
2. God's al- might- y pres- ence, he felt no sense of shame; The
3. By a might- y mir- a- cle they all were kept and fed;
4. Tim- brels rang,____ des- ert sands be- came a danc- ing floor; The
5. he came back to Fa- ther's house and Fa- ther took him in; He
6. Wine was flow- ing full and free, all mis- er- y was gone; The
7. want the bless- ings of the Lord but wor- ry what men say; Oh,
8. Men would leave their first love____ and turn to car- nal ways; But

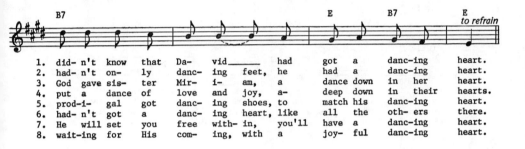

1.	Mi-	chol	thru	the	win-	dow	looked,	to	crit-	i-	cize	did	start,	She
2.	oil	of	glad-	ness	flowed	that	day,	it	quick-	ened	eve-	ry	part;	He
3.	Thru	the	Red	Sea	they	were	brought,	the	wa-	ters	stood a-	part,	And
4.	peo-	ple	sang	and	praised	God	there,	He	made	the	gloom de-	part,	And
5.	put	a	robe	up-	on	his	son,	the	mer-	ri-	ment	did	start,	The
6.	el-	der	broth-	er	look-	ing	on,	com-	plained	it	was-	n't	fair,	He
7.	let	the	Lord	have	full	con-	trol,	from	dead	tra-	di-	tions	part,	And
8.	true	born	saints	of	Je-	sus,	for	the	bride-	groom	set	a-	part,	Are

1.	did-	n't	know	that	Da-	vid	had	got	a	danc-	ing	heart.
2.	had-	n't	on-	ly	danc-	ing	feet,	he	had	a	danc-	ing	heart.
3.	God	gave	sis-	ter	Mir-	i-	am,	a	dance	down	in	her	heart.
4.	put	a	dance	of	love	and	joy,	a-	deep	down	in	their	hearts.
5.	prod-	i-	gal	got	danc-	ing	shoes,	to	match	his	danc-	ing	heart.
6.	had-	n't	got	a	danc-	ing	heart,	like	all	the	oth-	ers	there.
7.	He	will	set	you	free	with-	in,	you'll	have	a	danc-	ing	heart.
8.	wait-	ing	for	His	com-	ing,	with	a	joy-	ful	danc-	ing	heart.

Father, I Adore You

19

Words and Music by
Terrye Coelho

1.	Fa-	ther,	I a-	dore you,	lay my	life be-	fore you.	How I	love you.
2.	Je-	sus,	I a-	dore you,	lay my	life be-	fore you.	How I	love you.
3.	Spir-	it,	I a-	dore you,	lay my	life be-	fore you.	How I	love you.

Fill My House

20

from "Songs Of Brotherhood"
Words and Music by
Peter Kearney

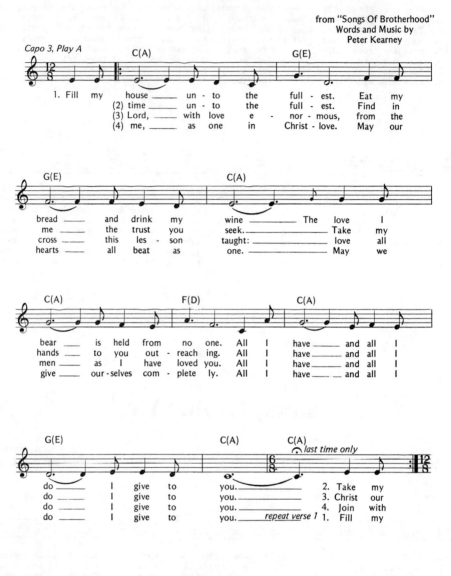

Adapted from
John 13

Words and Music by
Shirley Lewis Brown

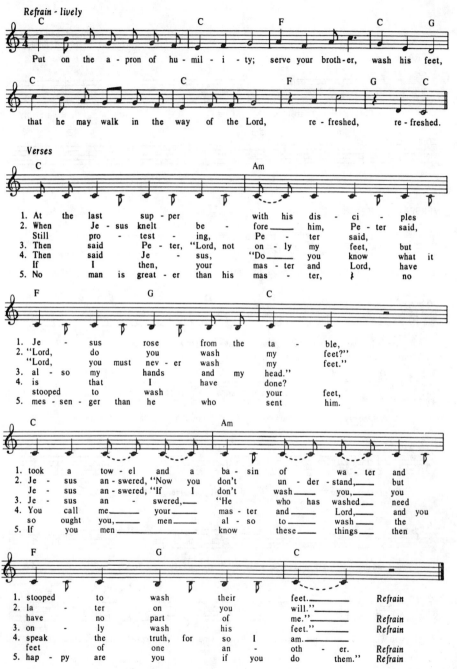

Refrain - lively

Put on the a-pron of hu-mil-i-ty; serve your broth-er, wash his feet,

that he may walk in the way of the Lord, re-freshed, re-freshed.

Verses

1. At the last sup-per with his dis-ci-ples
2. When Je-sus knelt be-fore him, Pe-ter said,
   Still pro-test-ing, Pe-ter said,
3. Then said Pe-ter, "Lord, not on-ly my feet, but
4. Then said Je-sus, "Do you know what it
   If I then, your mas-ter and Lord, have
5. No man is great-er than his mas-ter, no

1. Je-sus rose from the ta-ble,
2. "Lord, do you wash my feet?"
   "Lord, you must nev-er wash my feet."
3. al-so my hands and my head."
4. is that I have done?
   stooped to wash your feet,
5. mes-sen-ger than he who sent him.

1. took a tow-el and a ba-sin of wa-ter and
2. Je-sus an-swered, "Now you don't un-der-stand, but
   Je-sus an-swered, "If I don't wash you, you
3. Je-sus an-swered, "He who has washed need
4. You call me your mas-ter and Lord, and you
   so ought you, men al-so to wash the
5. If you men know these things then

1. stooped to wash their feet. *Refrain*
2. la-ter on you will." *Refrain*
   have no part of me." *Refrain*
3. on-ly wash his feet." *Refrain*
4. speak the truth, for so I am. *Refrain*
5. hap-py are you if you do them." *Refrain*

22
For You Are My God

Words and Music by
John B. Foley, S.J.

REFRAIN

For you are my God. You a - lone are my joy; de - fend me, O Lord.

VERSES

1. You give mar-vel-ous com-rades to me: the faith-ful who dwell in your land; those who choose a - li - en gods have cho-sen an a - li - en band.___

to refrain

2. You are my por-tion and cup; it is you that I claim for my prize. Your her - i - tage is my de - light: the lot you have giv - en to me.___

to refrain

3. Glad are my heart and my soul; se - cure-ly my bod - y shall rest. For you will not leave me for dead; nor lead your be - lov - ed a - stray.___

to refrain

4. You show me the path for my life; in your pres-ence the full-ness of joy. To be at your right hand for - ev - er for me would be hap-pi-ness al - ways.

Glorious God

23

Words and Music by
Sebastian Temple

VERSES Praise, hon-or, and glo-ry are yours. Praise, hon-or, and glo-ry are yours.

1. Glo - ri - ous God, _____ King of cre - a - tion, _____ we praise you, we
2. Glo - ri - ous God, _____ mag - ni - fi - cent, ho - ly, _____ we love you, a -
3. Glo - ri - ous God, _____ King of cre - a - tion, _____ we praise you, we

bless you, we wor-ship you in song; Glo - ri - ous God, _____ in ad - o
dore you, we come to you in prayer. Glo - ri - ous God, _____ might-y e -
bless you, we wor-ship you in song; Glo - ri - ous God, _____ in ad - o

ra - tion, _____ at your feet we be - long. _____ to refrain
ter - nal, _____ we sing your praise ev - 'ry - where. _____ to refrain
ra - tion, _____ at your feet we be - long. _____ to coda

REFRAIN

Lord of life, _____ Fa-ther al - might - y. Lord of hearts, _____

_____ Christ the King. _____ Lord of love, _____ Ho - ly

Spir - it, _____ to whom we hom - age bring. _____ to verse

Praise, hon-or, and glo-ry are yours. Praise hon-or and glo-ry are yours. _____

24 Glory to God

Words and Music by
Charles Christmas

REFRAIN
Capo 2, Play D

Ha - - le-lu-jah! Glo-ry to God in the high-est, and peace to Your peo-ple on earth._____ to verse

last time to Coda

VERSES

1. Fa - - - - - ther, O Fa-ther, all glo - ry__ be-longs_____ to You._____
2. Je - sus,_____ Je - sus, Je-sus,_____ we give_____ our hearts_____ to You._____
3. Spir- it,_____ Spir-it__ of God, Ho - ly coun-sel-lor,_____
4. With all the saints who have gone on__ be-fore us, with all___ of Your an - gels in cho-rus._____

1. Fa - ther,_____ lov-ing Fa - ther.
2. Be-lov-ed Son of God._____
3. teach-ing us_____ the things of God._____
4. We praise_____ Your Ho - ly name._____

to refrain

Glo- ry to God!_____

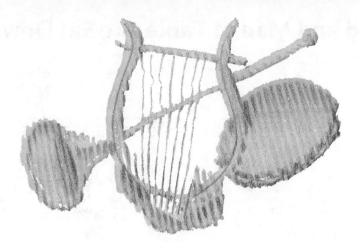

Glory to God, Glory   25

Words and Music by
Clarence Jos. Rivers

Capo 3, Play E

1 Praise Christ, the Son of the liv - ing God! *to refrain*

REFRAIN Glo - ry to God, glo - ry, O praise Him, al - le - lu - ia!

Glo - ry to God, glo - ry, O praise the name of the Lord!

2 Praise Christ, the Word of the liv - ing God! *to refrain*

3 Praise Christ, the Light of the liv - ing God! *to refrain*

26 God and Man at Table Are Sat Down

Words and Music by
Rev. Robert J. Stamps

Em | Bm | Em

1. O, wel-come all ye no - ble saints of old, _____ as
2. El - ders, mar - tyrs, all are fall - ing down; _____ as
3. Who is this who spreads the vic - t'ry feast? _____
4. Beg - gars, lame, and har - lots al - so here; _____ re-
5. Wor - ship in the pres - ence of the Lord, _____ with
6. When at last this earth shall pass a - way, _____ when

D | A7 | D | D7 | Em

now be - fore your ver - y eyes un - fold ____ the won - ders all so
proph-ets, pa - tri - archs are gath - 'ring 'round, ____ what an - gels longed to
Who is this who makes our war - ring cease? ____ Je - sus, Ris - en
pen - tant pub - li - cans are draw - ing near; ____ way - ward sons come
joy - ful songs and hearts in one ac - cord, ____ and let our Host at
Je - sus and His bride are one to stay, ____ the feast of love is

Continued ➤

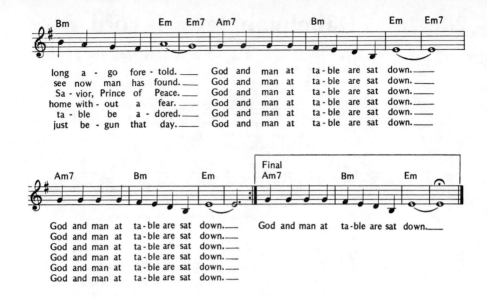

| Bm | | Em Em7 Am7 | | Bm | | Em Em7 |

long a - go fore - told. ___ God and man at ta - ble are sat down. ___
see now man has found. ___ God and man at ta - ble are sat down. ___
Sa - vior, Prince of Peace. ___ God and man at ta - ble are sat down. ___
home with - out a fear. ___ God and man at ta - ble are sat down. ___
ta - ble be a - dored. ___ God and man at ta - ble are sat down. ___
just be - gun that day. ___ God and man at ta - ble are sat down. ___

Am7 Bm Em **Final** Am7 Bm Em

God and man at ta - ble are sat down. ___ God and man at ta - ble are sat down. ___
God and man at ta - ble are sat down. ___
God and man at ta - ble are sat down. ___
God and man at ta - ble are sat down. ___
God and man at ta - ble are sat down. ___
God and man at ta - ble are sat down. ___

Hallelujah, I Want to Sing All About It 27

Words and Music by
Roy Turner

Hal- le- lu- jah, ___ I want to sing all a- bout it, Hal- le- lu- jah, ___ I want to

shout all a-bout it. Hal-le- lu- jah, ___ I can't live with-out ___ it, Praise God, ___ Praise

God; ___ Now I'm liv-ing in a new cre-a- tion, Now I'm drink-ing at the

well of sal-va- tion. Now there is no con- dem-na- tion, Praise God! ___

28 Hallelujah, Jesus Is Lord

M.A.F.

Mimi Armstrong Farra

With rhythmic boldness
Refrain

Hal - le - lu - jah!__ Hal - le - lu - jah!__
Hal - le - lu - jah!__ Hal - le - lu - jah!__

Hal - le - lu - jah!__ Je - sus is__ Lord!
Hal - le - lu - jah!__ Je - sus is__ King!__

Verse

1. All gath - er round the__ throne of the Lamb,
2. Lift up your voice with the thou - sands who cry,
3. Bless - ing and hon - or and glo - ry and pow'r,
4. All glo - ry be to the One Tri - une God,

Refrain

His prais - es sing through - out e - ter - ni - ty.
"Wor - thy, wor - thy art thou, Lamb of God."
be un - to him__ for - ev - er and ev - er.
the Fa - ther, Son, and the__ Ho - ly Spir - it.

29 He Is Lord

Words and Music by
Marvin V. Frey

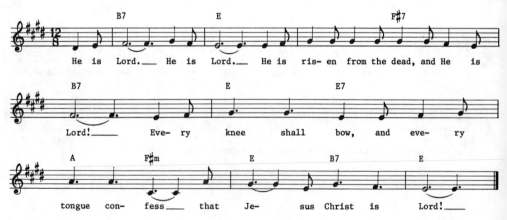

He is Lord.__ He is Lord.__ He is ris - en from the dead, and He is

Lord!__ Eve - ry knee shall bow, and eve - ry

tongue con - fess__ that Je - sus Christ is Lord!__

Here Comes Jesus

Unknown

Here comes Je- sus. See Him walk-ing on the wa- ter. He'll lift you up, and He'll help you to stand. Here comes Je- sus. He's the mas-ter of the waves that roll. Here comes Je- sus. He'll make you whole. Here comes

2nd time: D G D A   D D7 G D A D

3rd time: E A E B7   E E7 A E B7 E

4th time: F Bb F C   F F7 Bb F C F

5th time: G C G D   G G7 C G D G

FINAL ENDING

Here comes Je- sus. He'll make you whole.

Here comes Je- sus. He'll save your soul!

31 His Banner Over Me Is Love

Words and Music by
Alfred B. Smith

I'm my be-lov-ed's and He is mine. His ban-ner o-ver me is love.

I'm my be-lov-ed's and He is mine. His ban-ner o-ver me is love.

I'm my be-lov-ed's and He is mine. His ban-ner o-ver me is

love. His ban-ner o-ver me___ is love.___

Any of the following verses, or spontaneous verses, may also be used.

He fills me full of holy joy . . .
In Him I am a new creation . . .
He welcomes me to His banqueting table . . .
He lifts us up to heavenly places . . .
He makes straight paths before my feet . . .
/ Jesus is the rock of my salvation . . .
He calls us to the Body of Christ . . .
He builds His church on a firm foundation . . .
We hear Him say, "Lay down your life." . . .

How Great Is Our God

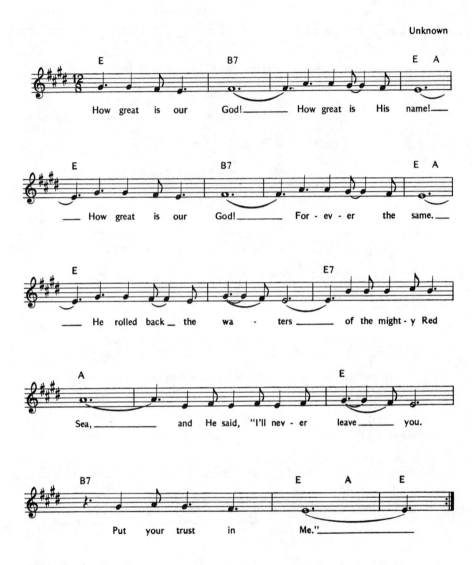

Unknown

How great is our God! How great is His name!

How great is our God! For-ev-er the same.

He rolled back the wa - ters of the might-y Red

Sea, and He said, "I'll nev - er leave you.

Put your trust in Me."

33 Hymn For a Prayer Meeting

Words and Music by
Ed Keefe
Mike Fitzgerald

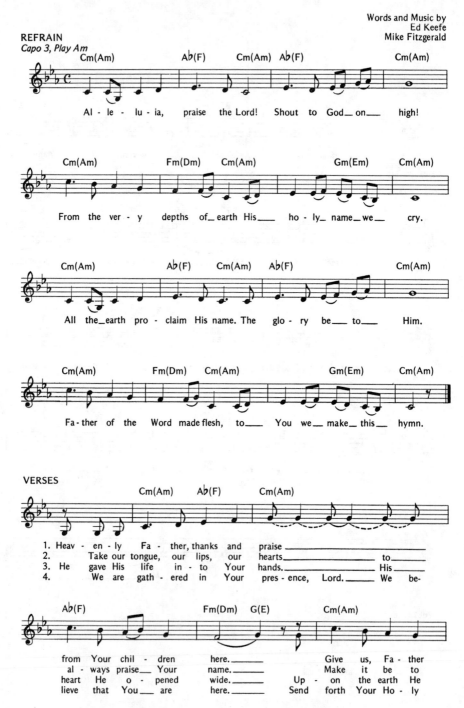

REFRAIN
Capo 3, Play Am

Al - le - lu - ia, praise the Lord! Shout to God_ on_ high!

From the ver - y depths of_ earth His_ ho - ly_ name_ we_ cry.

All the_earth pro - claim His name. The glo - ry be_ to_ Him.

Fa - ther of the Word made flesh, to_ You we_ make_ this_ hymn.

VERSES

1. Heav - en - ly Fa - ther, thanks and praise _____
2. Take our tongue, our lips, our hearts_____ to_
3. He gave His life in - to Your hands._____ His_
4. We are gath - ered in Your pres - ence, Lord. _____ We be-

from Your chil - dren here._____ Give us, Fa - ther
al - ways praise_ Your name._____ Make it be to
heart He o - pened wide._____ Up - on the earth He
lieve that You_ are here._____ Send forth Your Ho - ly

Fm(Dm)   Cm(Am)   A♭(F)   Cm(Am)   G(E)

of the_ Word, an ev - er lis - t'ning ear. Give us,
His re - nown; His prom - is - es we claim. He
poured His_ love, a flow - ing blood - red tide. In - to our
Spir - it, Lord, and help us all to share. Let Your

Cm(Am)   A♭(F)   Cm(Am)   A♭(F)   Fm(Dm) G(E)

Fa - ther, hearts of flesh;_____ let us be pierced__ through.___ Thus
prom - ised life, He prom - ised death, then life when death_ was through.___ He
hands He gives Him - self,_____ then gives us what_ to do;___
Spir - it build us up_____ in all we say_ or do,___ and

Cm(Am)   Fm(Dm)   Cm(Am)   Gm(Em)   Cm(Am)

make__ us, Fa - ther, like Your_ Son, Who is so much_ like__ You.
gives__ us ev - ery - thing He_ has, and all He has_ is __ You.
Share Him with all His broth - ers and give our selves_ to __ You.
keep__ us mind - ful of the_ fact: the glo - ry be_ to __ You.

to refrain

Hymn of Glory

Words and Music by
Charles Christmas

REFRAIN
Capo 3, Play A

Glo - ry ___ hal - le - lu jah!

Glo - ry ___ hal - le - lu - jah! ___

1. Give thanks to our God ___ and let him be praised, ___ with
2. His word ev - er true, ___ the Son of his love.
3. Wor - thy the Lamb who was slain for our sins. ___ He
4. Ho - ly ho - ly the Lord God Al - might - y who

sanc - ti - fied hearts ___ and hands that are raised. ___
Sing men of earth to the heav - ens a - bove.
laid down His life, ___ He rose up a - gain. ___
was, who is, ___ and who is to come. In

Come join a song ___ of praise to our God.
Hon - or and glo - ry be - long to our God.
To us He gives ___ un - end - ing life.
glo - ry come, ___ Lord Je - sus, come.

Hymn of the Universe

Words by
Ed Keefe

Music by
Mike Fitzgerald

VERSES

1. Who watch-es the wind as the birds fly out to greet the ris - ing___ sun? Who
2. Who watch-es the world as the sun rolls on to-charge the roar - ing___ stars? Who
3. Who pac-es the wave of a burst of light to make us all stand___ still? Who

watch-es the rain as the clouds pour in to meet the ris - en___ earth?
plays out the hymn of a spin - ning cloud to keep us on the___ run?
puls - es the note of a hun - dred hearts to move us on the___ march?

REFRAIN

Gal-ax - y build-er, Lord Je-sus the King, give us this day the bread that we need.

Feed us in heav-en the wheat of the fields. Give us to oth - ers in

FINAL ENDING

hun-dred-fold___ yields. ___ *to verse*   Gal-ax - y build-er, Lord Je-sus the King! ___

I Am the Bread of Life

Based on John 6 and 11

Words and Music by
Sr. M. Suzanne Toolan, S.M.

Capo 1, Play G

1. I am the bread of life; He who comes to me shall not hun-ger. He who be-lieves in me shall not thirst. No one can come to me un - less the Fa-ther draw him.

REFRAIN

And I will raise___ him up,___ and I will raise___ him up,___ and I will raise___ him up___ on the last___ day. day, and I will day.___

2. The bread that I will give is my flesh for the life of the world,___ and he who eats of this bread, he shall live for - ev - er, he shall live for - ev - er.

3. Un - less___ you eat of the flesh of the Son of Man, and drink of His blood, and drink of His blood, you shall not have life with - in you.

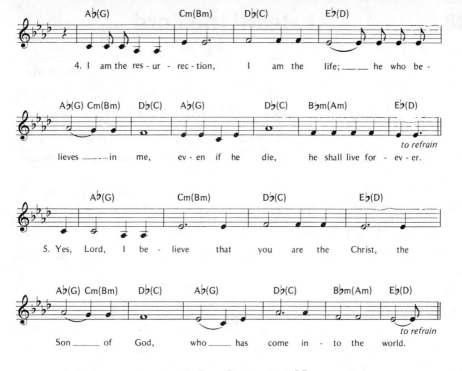

4. I am the res- ur - rec - tion, I am the life;_____ he who be-

lieves _____in me, ev - en if he die, he shall live for - ev - er.

to refrain

5. Yes, Lord, I be - lieve that you are the Christ, the

Son ____ of God, who ____ has come in - to the world.

to refrain

I Have Decided to Follow Jesus 37

Unknown

1. I have de- cid- ed_____ to fol- low Je- sus._____ I have de-
2. Though none go with me,_____ still I will fol- low._____ Though none go
3. The cross be- fore me,_____ the world be- hind me._____ The cross be-

cid- ed_____ to fol- low Je- sus._____ I have de- cid- ed____
with me,_____ still I will fol- low._____ Though none go with me,___
fore me,_____ the world be- hind me._____ The cross be- fore me,___

____ to fol- low Je- sus._____ No turn-ing back,___ no turn-ing back!___
____ still I will fol- low._____ No turn-ing back,___ no turn-ing back!___
____ the world be- hind me._____ No turn-ing back,___ no turn-ing back!___

I Heard the Lord

Words and Music by
Jacob Krieger

Capo 4, Play C

I heard the Lord call my name. Lis-ten close, you'll hear the same. I heard the Lord call my name. Lis-ten close, you'll hear the same. I heard the Lord call my name. Lis-ten close, you'll hear the same. Take His hand; we are glo-ry bound. His word is love; love's his word: that's the mes - sage that I heard. His word is love; love's His word: that's the mes - sage that I heard. His word is love; love's His word: that's the mes - sage that I heard. Take His hand; we are glory bound. Place your hand in His and you will know; He will show you where to go.

39 I Want to Walk as a Child of the Light

Words and Music by
Kathleen Thomerson

VERSES

1. I want to walk as a child of the light. I want to fol- low
2. I want to see the bright-ness of God. I want to look at
3. I'm look- ing for the com- ing of Christ. I want to be with

Je- sus. God set the stars to give light to the world. The
Je- sus. Clear sun of right-eous- ness, shine on my path, and
Je- sus. When we have run with pa- tience the race, we

REFRAIN

star of my life is Je- sus.
show me the way to the Fa- ther. In Him there is no dark-ness at
shall know the joy of Je- sus.

all, the night and the day are both a- like. The Lamb is the light of the

cit- y of God. Shine in my heart, Lord Je- sus. A- men.

to verse

40 I Will Arise

Words and Music by
Mimi Armstrong Farra

Refrain

I will a- rise so ear- ly in the morn- ing,

rise to sing my Sa- vior's prais- es;

After the last refrain, the refrain and verse two may be sung
simultaneously observing the Coda

41 I Will Sing of the Mercies of the Lord

J. H. Fillmore

I will sing of the mer- cies of the Lord for- ev- er, I will

sing, I will sing. I will sing of the mer- cies of the Lord.

With my mouth__ will I make known Thy faith- ful- ness, Thy faith-ful-ness. With my

mouth__ will I make known Thy faith- ful-ness to all gen- er- a-tions. I will

42 In My Father's House

Unknown

1. Come and go with me to my Fa-ther's house, to my Father's house,

to my Fa- ther's house. Come and go with me

to my Fa- ther's house, where there's joy, joy, joy!

Any of the following verses, or spontaneous verses, may be used.

2. It's not very far to my Father's house . . .
3. Jesus is the Way to my Father's house . . .
4. Jesus is the Light in my Father's house . . .
5. All is peace and love in my Father's house . . .
6. We will dance and sing in my Father's house . . .
7. We will praise the Lord in my Father's house . . .

43 Israel, Rely on Yahweh

based on Psalm 130(131), M.F.

Mike Fitzgerald

REFRAIN
Capo 3, Play A

Is- ra- el, re- ly on Yah- weh now and for- ev- er- more.___ *to verse*

VERSES

1. Yah-weh, my heart is not am- bi- tious. My eyes do not
2. I am not con-cerned with great- ness or mar- vels be-

look too high. *to refrain* 3. E- nough for me to keep my soul
yond my scope. 4. Glo- ry be to the Fa- ther Al-

tran- quil like a Child in its moth- er's arms,
might-y, to the Son and Spir- it praise,

as con- tent as a child that has been weaned.
[OMIT] e- ter- nal praise in end- less peace.

to refrain

44 It Is Good to Give Thanks to the Lord

Psalm 91 (92)

Music by
Robert Twynham

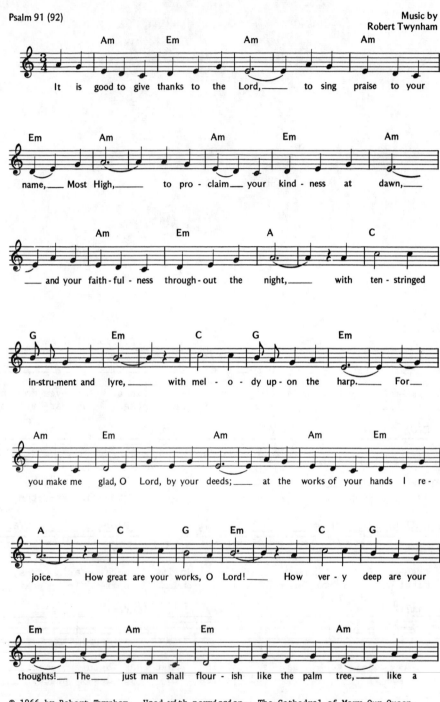

It is good to give thanks to the Lord,——— to sing praise to your name,——— Most High,——— to pro - claim——— your kind - ness at dawn,——— —— and your faith - ful - ness through - out the night,——— with ten - stringed in-stru-ment and lyre, ——— with mel - o - dy up-on the harp.——— For—— you make me glad, O Lord, by your deeds;——— at the works of your hands I re-joice.——— How great are your works, O Lord!——— How ver - y deep are your thoughts!—— The—— just man shall flour - ish like the palm tree,——— like a

It's a Brand New Day

45

P.Q.

Paul Quinlan

1. It's a brand new day,_____ ev - 'ry - thing is fine._____
2. Well the heav'ns de - clare_____ in a way so grand;_____
3. His law of love,_____ it is whol - ly wise._____

_____ Though it may be gray, I want you to know that the sun's gon - na
_____ If the skies are fair or wind - y or gray, it's the work of His
_____ Word_____ from a - bove gives joy to my heart and it's light to my

shine._____ And out of that sky,_____ pierc - ing ev - er - y cloud_____
hands._____ And down on that ground,_____ with_____ nev - er a word,_____
eyes._____ It's rich - es are fine_____ out_____ last - ing all days_____

_____ is our God on high._____ There will be a new heart for ev - er - y
_____ such a might - y sound._____ And the morn - ing will see the roll - ing
_____ to the end of time._____ Though I walk in the path of e - vil

man like the flow - ers that come in ear - ly Spring. For ev - er - y
sun as he hap - pi - ly ris - es o'er the land; A mes - sen - ger
ways and my thoughts are a pres - ence caus - ing pain There's al - ways the

life there is_____ a plan no mat - ter what au - tumn breez - es bring.
on his dai - ly run bring news of a Fa - ther's guid - ing hand.
sun of fu - ture days that fol - lows a time of wind and rain.

So put a - way cares, let free - dom be yours. Joy is ev - er - y - where,

joy is ev - er - y - where._____ Let free - dom ring, Al - le - lu - ia now

ev - 'ry - bod - y_____ sing, let our voi - ces shout to a might - y King.

46

Jacob's Song

Words and Music by
Jacob Krieger

Capo 4, Play C

Sing praise to the Lord for-ev-er and ev-er.

Sing praise to the Lord for-

Call un-to Him for hope in sal-va-tion.

ev-er and ev-er. Call un-to Him for

Sing praise al-le-lu-ia, sing praise al-le-lu. Sing

hope in sal-va-tion. Sing praise al-le-lu-ia, sing praise al-le-lu. Sing

Fine

praise al-le-lu-ia, sing praise, al-le-lu. Call un-to Him. Call un-

Fine

praise al-le-lu-ia, sing praise al-le-lu. Call un-to Him. Call un-

to His name. Sing praise to the Lamb, for life ev-er-last-

to His name. Sing

ing. Call un-to Je-sus, call un-to the

praise to the Lamb, for life ev-er-last-ing.

Jesus in the Morning 47

Words and Music by
Marvin V. Frey

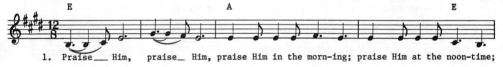

1. Praise__ Him, praise__ Him, praise Him in the morn-ing; praise Him at the noon-time;

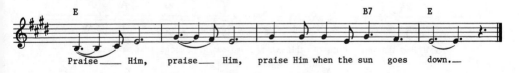

Praise__ Him, praise__ Him, praise Him when the sun goes down.__

Any of the following verses, or spontaneous verses, may also be used.

2. Jesus, Jesus, Jesus in the morning . . .
3. Serve Him, serve Him, serve Him in the morning . . .
4. Love Him, love Him, love Him in the morning . . .
5. Thank Him, thank Him, thank Him in the morning . . .

48 Jesus Is the One Who Saves

Words and Music by
James Berlucchi

1. All glo-ry to the Fa-ther of life.___ Praise be to the Ho-ly Spir - it, ___ and to the shin-ing light of this world.___ Je-sus is the one who saves.___

2. You're the first-born of all of the sons, ___ king___ of the new cre-a - tion.___ You're the bro-ther who makes us all one.___ Je-sus is the one who saves.___

3. Thank you Je-sus for ris-ing for us, ___ the Fa-ther's love com-plete and glo - rious. ___ Now we claim the vic-t'ry You give to us.___ Je-sus is the one who saves. ___

4. Just call up-on the name of the Lord.___ Ask Him for His Ho-ly Spir - it. ___ You'll find the one truth of this world.___ Je-sus is the one who saves.___

Je - sus is the one who saves.___ Je-sus is the one who saves. ___

The King of Glory

Words by
Fr. Willard Jabusch

Israeli Folk Melody

REFRAIN

The King of glo- ry comes, the na- tion re- joi- ces.

O- pen the gates be- fore him, lift up your voi- ces.

VERSES

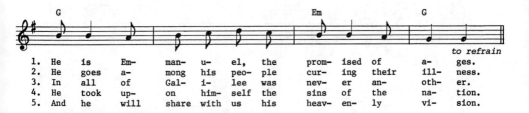

1. Who	is	the	king of	glo-	ry;	how	shall we	call him?
2. In	all	of	Gal- i-	lee,	in	cit-	y or	vil- lage,
3. Sing then	of	Da-	vid's Son,	our	Sav-	ior and	broth-er;
4. He	gave	his	life for	us,	the	pledge of	sal-	va- tion,
5. He con-	quered	sin and	death; he	tru-	ly	has	ris- en.

to refrain

1. He	is	Em-	man- u-	el,	the	prom-	ised of	a- ges.
2. He	goes	a-	mong his	peo-	ple	cur-	ing their	ill- ness.
3. In	all	of	Gal- i-	lee was	nev-	er an-	oth- er.
4. He	took	up-	on him-	self	the	sins	of the	na- tion.
5. And	he	will	share with	us	his	heav-	en- ly	vi- sion.

50 King of Kings

Words and Music by
Charles Christmas

1. In__ the be-gin - ning, the Word__ of God__ came, cre - a - ting ev-'ry-

thing by call - ing its__ name. "Let there be__ light, and call it__ the__

day. Let there__ be__ night. Oh hear and o - bey."

REFRAIN

He's the King of Kings. He's the Lord_____ of Lords. _____ He's the

mas - ter of ev - 'ry - thing. Let__ Him be a - dored._____ *to verse*

2. And the Word,__ He made man as the crown of cre-a - tion,__ but man,__ he__

fell in - to sin __ and sep-a - ra - tion. So the Word__ be-came__ flesh in

space___ and___ time, bring-ing sal - va-tion to all___ man-kind.
to refrain

3. Oh, Je - sus, you are the lov-ing Sav-ior. Je -

sus, you are the way for us. Oh, wor-ship the King for there

is___ no___ oth-er.___ To Him___ sing; He's your Lord___ and broth-er.
to refrain

After the final verse, the refrain may be repeated using the words "You're the King of Kings.
You're the Lord of Lords. You're the master of everything. May you be adored."

Let All That Is Within Me   51

Translation by
Melvin Harrel

Composer Unknown

Let all that is with-in me___ cry, "Ho-ly!" Let all that is with-in me___ cry,

"Ho- ly!" Ho- ly! Ho- ly! Ho- ly! Ho- ly is the Lamb that was slain.___

This song may be sung substituting "Worthy," "Jesus," or "Glory" for "Holy."

The Light of Christ

Words and Music by
Donald Fishel

REFRAIN

The light of Christ has come in-to the world, the
The light of Christ has come in - to the world,

light of Christ has come in-to the world.
the light of Christ has come.

Continued ▶

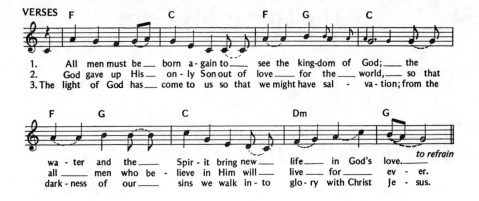

VERSES

1. All men must be born a-gain to see the king-dom of God; the
2. God gave up His on-ly Son out of love for the world, so that
3. The light of God has come to us so that we might have sal - va-tion; from the

wa - ter and the Spir - it bring new life in God's love.
all men who be - lieve in Him will live for ev - er.
dark - ness of our sins we walk in - to glo - ry with Christ Je - sus.

to refrain

Litany

53

Words and Music by
Rev. Carey Landry

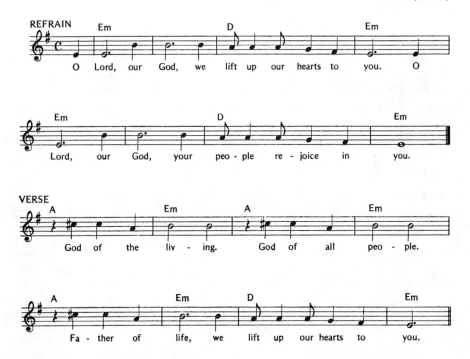

REFRAIN

O Lord, our God, we lift up our hearts to you. O
Lord, our God, your peo - ple re - joice in you.

VERSE

God of the liv - ing. God of all peo - ple.
Fa - ther of life, we lift up our hearts to you.

Verses may be improvised using the above melody, as on album W/G 7302 from The Word of God.

54   The Lord Is My Light

Psalm 27:1

Music by
Pauline M. Mills

The Lord Is Present in His Sanctuary 55

Words and Music by
Gail Cole

1. The Lord is pres-ent in His sanc- tu-ar- y, Let us praise the Lord! The
2. The Lord is pres-ent in His sanc- tu-ar- y, Let us sing to the Lord! The
3. The Lord is pres-ent in His sanc- tu-ar- y, Let us de-light in the Lord! The
4. The Lord is pres-ent in His sanc- tu-ar- y, Let us love the Lord! The

Lord is pres-ent in His peo- ple gath- ered here, Let us praise the Lord!
Lord is pres-ent in His peo- ple gath- ered here, Let us sing to the Lord!
Lord is pres-ent in His peo- ple gath- ered here, Let us de-light in the Lord! De-
Lord is pres-ent in His peo- ple gath- ered here, Let us love the Lord!

Praise Him, Praise Him! Let us praise the Lord!
Sing to Him, Sing to Him! Let us sing to the Lord!
light in Him, De- light in Him! Let us de- light in the Lord! De-
Love Him, Love Him! Let us love the Lord!

Praise Him, Praise Him! Let us praise Je- sus!
Sing to Him, Sing to Him! Let us sing to Je- sus!
light in Him, De- light in Him! Let us de-light in Je- sus!
Love Him, Love Him! Let us love Je- sus!

56 Love

Music by
Jean Goeboro

I Cor. 13

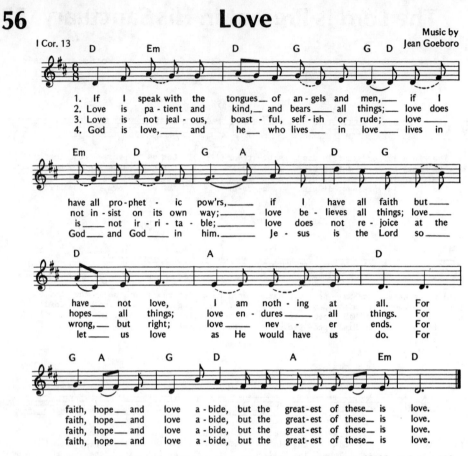

1. If I speak with the tongues of an-gels and men, if I have all pro-phet - ic pow'rs, if I have all faith but have not love, I am noth-ing at all. For faith, hope and love a - bide, but the great-est of these is love.

2. Love is pa - tient and kind, and bears all things; love does not in - sist on its own way; love be - lieves all things; love hopes all things; love en - dures all things. For faith, hope and love a - bide, but the great-est of these is love.

3. Love is not jeal - ous, boast - ful, self - ish or rude; love is not ir - ri - ta - ble; love does not re - joice at the wrong, but right; love nev - er ends. For faith, hope and love a - bide, but the great-est of these is love.

4. God is love, and he who lives in love lives in God and God in him. Je - sus is the Lord so let us love as He would have us do. For faith, hope and love a - bide, but the great-est of these is love.

57 The Love Round

Unknown

Love, love, love, love. Chris- tians, this is your call:

only on repeats

Love your neigh- bor as your- self, for God loves us all.

Optional verse: Jesus, Jesus, let me tell You how I feel:
You have given me Your riches; I love You so.

My Soul Doth Magnify the Lord

Luke 1: 46, 47, 49

Unknown

My soul doth mag-ni-fy the Lord, and my spir-it hath re-joiced in God my Sa-vior, for___ He that is might-y hath done great things; and ho-ly is His name. My soul doth mag-ni-fy the Lord, my soul doth mag-ni-fy the Lord, and my spir-it hath re-joiced in God my Sa-vior, for___ He that is might-y hath done great things; and ho-ly is His name.

O Come, Let Us Adore Him

Latin, 18th c.
Tr. by Fr. Oakeley (1802–1880)
(and others)

Adeste Fidelis
Cantus Diversi by
J. F. Wade (1710–1786)

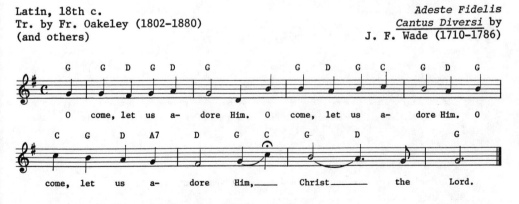

O come, let us a- dore Him. O come, let us a- dore Him. O come, let us a- dore Him,___ Christ____ the Lord.

The following verses, or spontaneous verses, may also be used.

For He alone is worthy.
And He shall come in glory.

60 Praise My God With the Tambourine

First Chorus in Unison; others in parts.

Boldly, with vigor
Chorus

Words and Music by
Diane Davis

Praise my God with the tam-bou-rine; sing to the Lord with the

Last time only Verse

1. Am 2. Am MEN:

cym - bals. bals. 1. I will sing a new song to

my God. "You are great, You are glo - ri - ous, won-der-ful-ly___ strong." *To Chorus*

WOMEN:

2. "May your whole cre - a - tion serve you. When you speak, things come___

___ in - to being; no one can re - sist your___ voice."

ALL:

3. "Should the moun-tains top - ple to min - gle with the waves, should rocks melt like wax be -

- fore your face, to those who fear you, you would still be___ mer - ci - ful." *To Chorus*

61 Psalm 89

Words and Music by
Karen Barrie

1. I have made a cov-e-nant with my cho-sen, giv-en my ser-vant my word. —

I have made your name to last for - ev - er, built to out - last all time. ___

REFRAIN

I will cel - e - brate your love for-ev-er, Yah - weh. Age on age, ___ my

62 Psalm 145

Words and Music by
Charles Christmas

REFRAIN
Capo 3, Play A

I will ex-tol You, my God and King, and bless Your name for- ev- er.

Eve- ry day I will bless You and praise Your name for- ev- er. Great is the Lord and

great-ly to be praised, and His great-ness is un- search- a- ble.

to Coda
after last verse

to verse

VERSES

1. I will de- clare Your great- ness and Your glo- ri-ous maj- es-
2. All Your works shall thank You, and all Your saints shall
3. The eyes of all look to You, and You o- pen up Your

ty. Men will pro-claim Your might-y acts and sing of Your right-eous-
bless you. They shall speak of Your glo- ry and tell of Your
hand. You sat- is- fy all de- sire of ev- ery liv- ing

ness. For the Lord is gra- cious, and He is mer- ci-
pow'r. You, O Lord, are faith- ful in all Your words and
thing. You are just in all Your ways and near to all who

ful, al- ways a- bound- ing in stead- fast love.
deeds. You up- hold the fall- ing and raise those bowed down.
call. You hear their cry and save all those who love You.

to refrain

Let us praise our God!

Rejoice Always

I Thes. 5:16–18

Music by
Tom and Ellen Gryniewicz

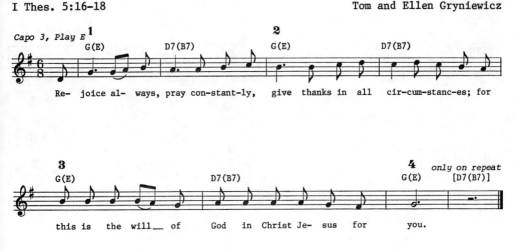

Re- joice al- ways, pray con-stant-ly, give thanks in all cir-cum-stanc-es; for

this is the will— of God in Christ Je- sus for you.

Rejoice in the Lord Always

Philippians 4:4

by Evelyn Tarner

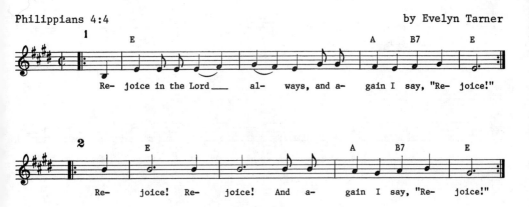

Re- joice in the Lord— al- ways, and a- gain I say, "Re- joice!"

Re- joice! Re- joice! And a- gain I say, "Re- joice!"

65 Romans Eight

Words by E. Garzilli
Based on Romans 8:28-38

Music by
Enrico Garzilli

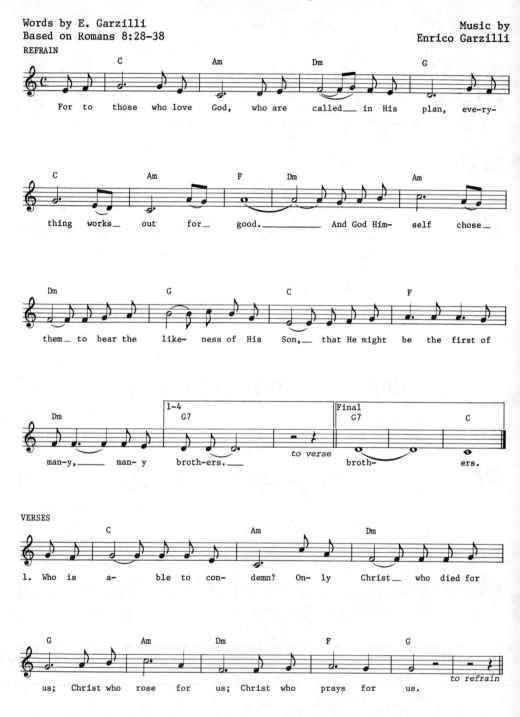

REFRAIN

For to those who love God, who are called— in His plan, eve-ry-thing works— out for— good.———— And God Him- self chose— them— to bear the like- ness of His Son,— that He might be the first of man-y,——— man- y broth-ers.— *to verse* broth- ers.

1-4 G7 | Final G7 C

VERSES

1. Who is a- ble to con- demn? On- ly Christ— who died for us; Christ who rose for us; Christ who prays for us. *to refrain*

66 Seek Ye First/Matt. 6:33

Music by
Karen Lafferty

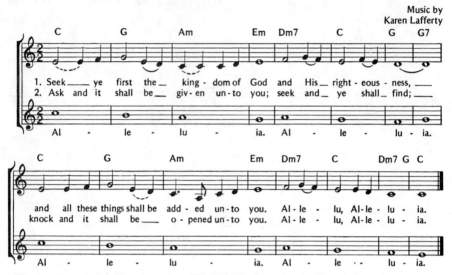

C	G	Am	Em Dm7	C	G G7

1. Seek ___ ye first the ___ king - dom of God and His ___ right - eous - ness, ___
2. Ask and it shall be ___ giv - en un - to you; seek and ___ ye shall ___ find; ___

Al - le - lu - ia. Al - le - lu - ia.

C	G	Am	Em Dm7	C	Dm7 G C

and all these things shall be add - ed un - to you. Al - le - lu, Al - le - lu - ia.
knock and it shall be ___ o - pened un - to you. Al - le - lu, Al - le - lu - ia.

Al - le - lu - ia. Al - le - lu - ia.

The second verse included here is not part of "Seek Ye First" as written by Karen Lafferty.
Its origin is unknown.

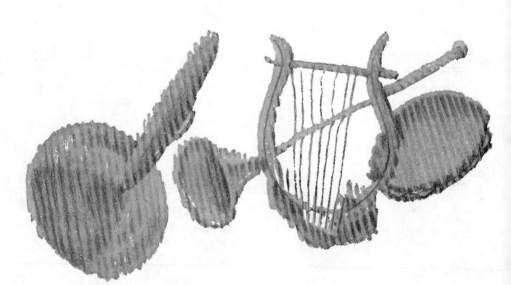

Sing to God a Brand New Canticle

Based on Psalm 149, P.Q.

Paul Quinlan

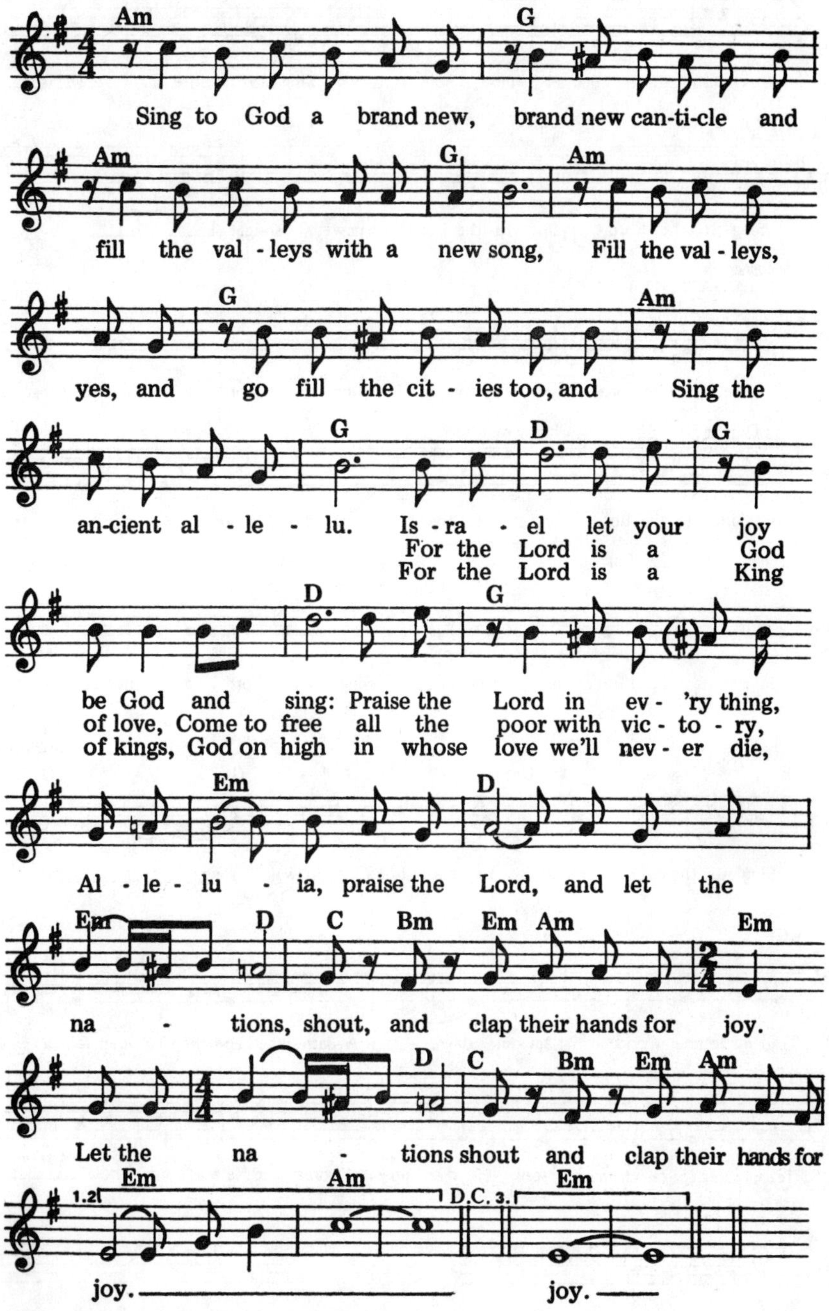
Sing to God a brand new, brand new can-ti-cle and
fill the val - leys with a new song, Fill the val - leys,
yes, and go fill the cit - ies too, and Sing the
an-cient al - le - lu. Is - ra - el let your joy
For the Lord is a God
For the Lord is a King
be God and sing: Praise the Lord in ev - 'ry thing,
of love, Come to free all the poor with vic - to - ry,
of kings, God on high in whose love we'll nev - er die,
Al - le - lu - ia, praise the Lord, and let the
na - tions, shout, and clap their hands for joy.
Let the na - tions shout and clap their hands for
joy.
joy.
1.2
D.C. 3.

The music is available in the songbook, Songs of Praise and Reconciliation, and from It's a Brand New Day! (record, songbook, and sheet music) from North American Liturgy Resources.

68 Sing to the Lord

Words and Music by
Donald Fishel

INTRODUCTION *Slowly*

Sing to the Lord a new song. Sing to the Lord a new song.

Sing to the Lord, sing to the Lord a new song.

A little faster

Sing to the Lord a new song. Sing to the Lord a new song.

Sing to the Lord, sing to the Lord a new song.

REFRAIN *Moderately fast*

Sing to the Lord a new song. Sing to the Lord a new song.

to Coda after fourth verse

Sing to the Lord, sing to the Lord a new song.

VERSES

1. God made the world in seven days. A-dam sinned and then all men fell a-way.

Je-sus came to re-deem my soul. He died up-on the cross, and He made me whole!

to refrain

2. God said to Mo-ses, "Go and set My peo-ple free. I will be your guide, just

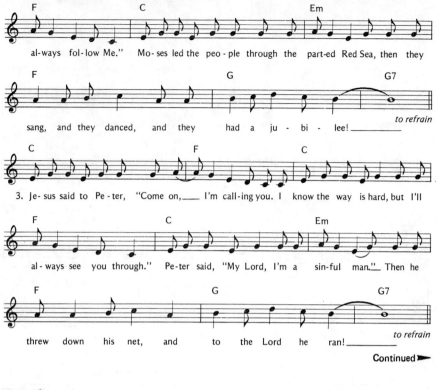

al - ways fol - low Me." Mo - ses led the peo - ple through the part - ed Red Sea, then they

sang, and they danced, and they had a ju - bi - lee! _____

to refrain

3. Je - sus said to Pe - ter, "Come on, ___ I'm call - ing you. I know the way is hard, but I'll

al - ways see you through." Pe - ter said, "My Lord, I'm a sin - ful man." Then he

threw down his net, and to the Lord he ran! _____

to refrain

Continued ▶

Song of Good News

Words by
Fr. Willard Jabusch

Israeli Folk Melody

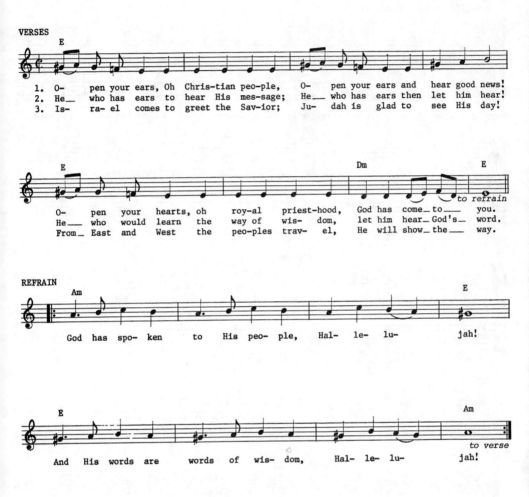

VERSES

1. O- pen your ears, Oh Chris-tian peo-ple, O- pen your ears and hear good news!
2. He__ who has ears to hear His mes-sage; He__ who has ears then let him hear!
3. Is- ra- el comes to greet the Sav-ior; Ju- dah is glad to see His day!

O- pen your hearts, oh roy-al priest-hood, God has come__ to__ you.
He__ who would learn the way of wis- dom, let him hear__ God's__ word.
From__ East and West the peo-ples trav- el, He will show__ the__ way.

to refrain

REFRAIN

God has spo- ken to His peo- ple, Hal- le- lu- jah!

And His words are words of wis- dom, Hal- le- lu- jah!

to verse

70 The Song of Moses

Words by B. C. Pulkingham
Based on Exodus 15

Words and Music by
Betty Carr Pulkingham

REFRAIN
Capo 2, Play Am
DESCANT *only after fourth verse*

MELODY

Lord is my strength and song, and He is be-come my sal-
The Lord is my strength and song, and He is be-come my sal-

va-tion. He is my God and I will pre-pare Him an
va-tion. He is my God and I will pre-pare Him an

hab-i-ta-tion, my fa-ther's God and I will ex-alt Him.
hab-i-ta-tion, my fa-ther's God and I will ex-alt Him. *to verse*

1. He hath tri-umphed glo-rious-ly, I will sing un-to the Lord. He hath tri-umphed
glo-rious-ly, the horse and his ri-der hath He thrown in the sea. *to refrain*

2. The Lord is a man of war, the Lord is His name. Pha-roh's char-iots
and his host hath He cast, hath He cast in-to the sea! *to refrain*

3. Thy right hand, O Lord, is be- come glo- ri- ous in pow'r.

Thy right hand, O Lord, hath cast in piec- es the en- e- my.

to refrain

4. Who is like un-to Thee, O Lord,— a- mong the gods? Who is like Thee,

glo-rious in ho- li-ness, fear-ful in prais- es, do- ing won- ders? The

D.S. al Coda

Continued ►

The Spirit and the Bride

71

Based on Revelation 22:12–17

Words and Music by
Charles Christmas

REFRAIN

The Spir-it and the bride say, "Come." Let all who hear say, "Come." Let
him who is thirst-y come take the wa-ter of life with-out price.

to Coda after last verse
to verse

VERSES

1. Be-hold, I am com-ing soon bring-ing my re-ward. I am the Al-pha and the O-me-ga, the first and the last, the be-gin-ing and the end.
2. Blessed are all who wash their robes to eat from the tree of life, and en-ter the cit-y by the gates. I am the off-spring of Da-vid, the bright and morn-ing star.
3. If an-y man thirst, let him come to me, and let him drink, and out of his heart there shall flow streams of liv-ing wa-ter. This is the Spir-it; just ask and re-ceive.

E-ven so, come, Lord Je-sus! Come, Lord Je-sus!

72

The Spirit Is A-Movin'

Words and Music by
Carey Landry
Pentecost, 1967

Quick tempo, but steady.

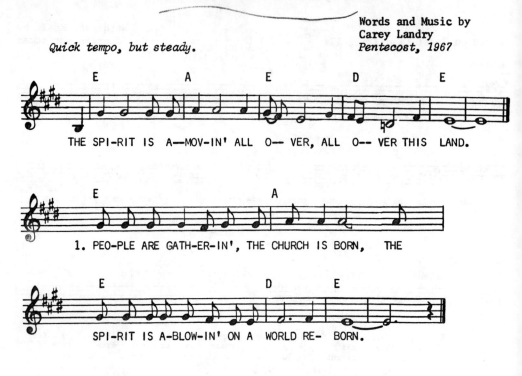

THE SPI-RIT IS A—MOV-IN' ALL O—VER, ALL O—VER THIS LAND.

1. PEO-PLE ARE GATH-ER-IN', THE CHURCH IS BORN, THE

SPI-RIT IS A-BLOW-IN' ON A WORLD RE- BORN.

2. Doors are opening as the Spirit comes,
   His fire is burning in his people now.

3. Filled with the Spirit we are sent to serve,
   We are called out as brothers, we are called to work.

4. The world, born once, is born again,
   We re-create it in love and joy.

5. Old men are dreaming dreams,
   And young men see the light.

6. Old walls are falling down,
   And men are speaking with each other.

7. The Spirit fills us with his power
   To be his witnesses to all we meet.

8. The Spirit urges us to travel light
   To be men of courage who spread his fire.

9. God has poured out his Spirit
   On all--on all of mankind.

Spirit of the Living God — 73

Adapted from "Spirit Of the Living God"
Words and Music by
Daniel Iverson

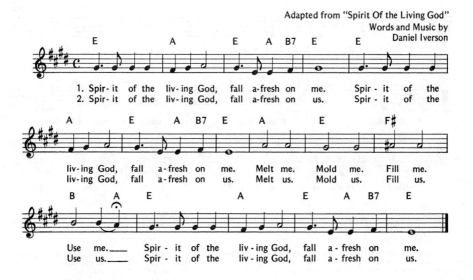

1. Spir-it of the liv-ing God, fall a-fresh on me. Spir-it of the living God, fall a-fresh on me. Melt me. Mold me. Fill me. Use me.___ Spir-it of the liv-ing God, fall a-fresh on me.

2. Spir-it of the liv-ing God, fall a-fresh on us. Spir-it of the living God, fall a-fresh on us. Melt us. Mold us. Fill us. Use us.___ Spir-it of the liv-ing God, fall a-fresh on us.

74 There Is None Like Him

C.J.R.

Clarence Jos. Rivers

Capo 1, Play E

4 He was born of a Vir-gin, And He lived as a com-mon man, Yet none the less our God, O there is none like Him.

Refrain

5 He was the God im-mor-tal, Yet He died up-on a cross, And in dy-ing He slew death. O there is none like Him.

Refrain

6 He was the Lord al-might-y, Yet He did not use His pow-er, And His weak-ness was like strength. O there is none like Him.

Refrain

7 He lived with us, He died for us, He made Him-self our food, We are mem-bers of His Bo-dy. There is none like Him.

Refrain

75

There's a River of Life

Verses two through six by
Betty Carr Pulkingham

Music and verse one by
L. Casebolt

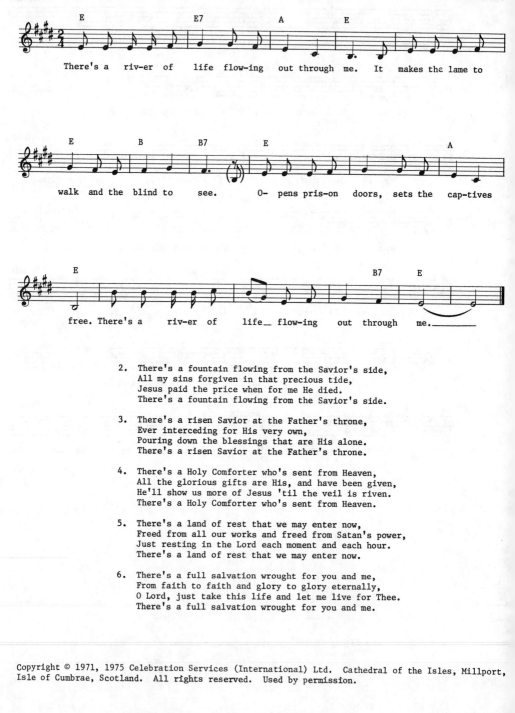

There's a riv-er of life flow-ing out through me. It makes the lame to walk and the blind to see. O-pens pris-on doors, sets the cap-tives free. There's a riv-er of life flow-ing out through me.

2. There's a fountain flowing from the Savior's side,
   All my sins forgiven in that precious tide,
   Jesus paid the price when for me He died.
   There's a fountain flowing from the Savior's side.

3. There's a risen Savior at the Father's throne,
   Ever interceding for His very own,
   Pouring down the blessings that are His alone.
   There's a risen Savior at the Father's throne.

4. There's a Holy Comforter who's sent from Heaven,
   All the glorious gifts are His, and have been given,
   He'll show us more of Jesus 'til the veil is riven.
   There's a Holy Comforter who's sent from Heaven.

5. There's a land of rest that we may enter now,
   Freed from all our works and freed from Satan's power,
   Just resting in the Lord each moment and each hour.
   There's a land of rest that we may enter now.

6. There's a full salvation wrought for you and me,
   From faith to faith and glory to glory eternally,
   O Lord, just take this life and let me live for Thee.
   There's a full salvation wrought for you and me.

They That Wait Upon the Lord 76

Based on Isaiah 40:31

Words and Music by
Stuart Hamblen

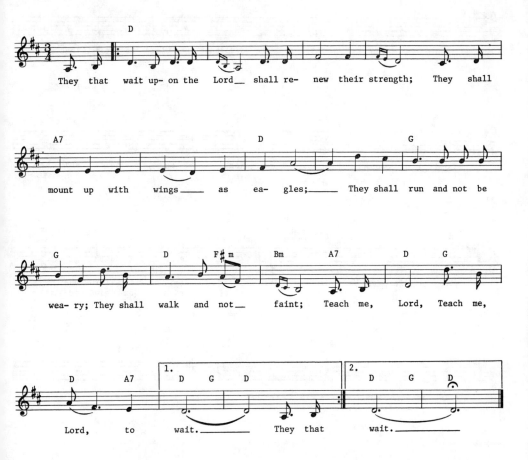

They that wait up- on the Lord__ shall re- new their strength; They shall
mount up with wings____ as ea- gles;____ They shall run and not be
wea- ry; They shall walk and not__ faint; Teach me, Lord, Teach me,
Lord, to wait.____ They that wait.____

This Is the Day

Psalm 118:24

Unknown

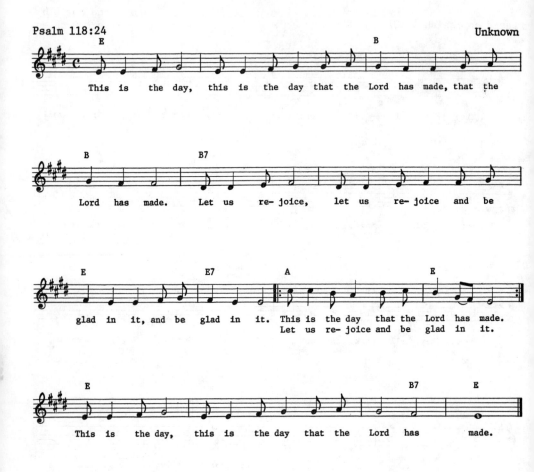

This is the day, this is the day that the Lord has made, that the

Lord has made. Let us re-joice, let us re-joice and be

glad in it, and be glad in it. This is the day that the Lord has made.
Let us re-joice and be glad in it.

This is the day, this is the day that the Lord has made.

Copyright unknown

We See the Lord

Verses two, three, and four by
James E. Byrne

Unknown

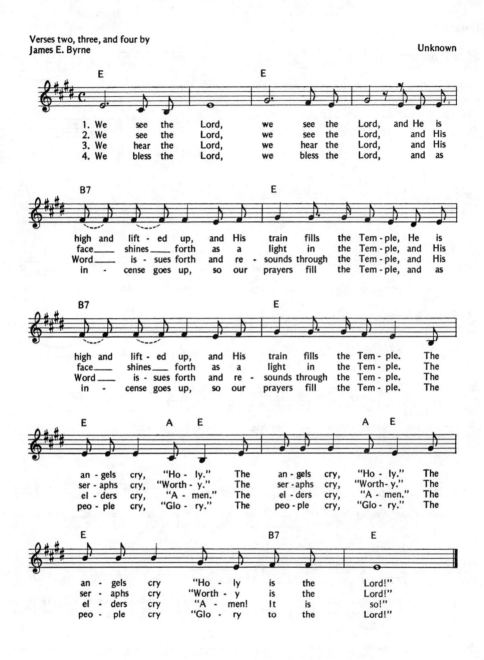

1. We see the Lord, we see the Lord, and He is
2. We see the Lord, we see the Lord, and His
3. We hear the Lord, we hear the Lord, and His
4. We bless the Lord, we bless the Lord, and as

high and lift - ed up, and His train fills the Tem - ple, He is
face___ shines ___ forth as a light in the Tem - ple, and His
Word___ is - sues forth and re - sounds through the Tem - ple, and His
in - cense goes up, so our prayers fill the Tem - ple, and as

high and lift - ed up, and His train fills the Tem - ple. The
face___ shines ___ forth as a light in the Tem - ple. The
Word___ is - sues forth and re - sounds through the Tem - ple. The
in - cense goes up, so our prayers fill the Tem - ple. The

an - gels cry, "Ho - ly." The an - gels cry, "Ho - ly." The
ser - aphs cry, "Worth - y." The ser - aphs cry, "Worth - y." The
el - ders cry, "A - men." The el - ders cry, "A - men." The
peo - ple cry, "Glo - ry." The peo - ple cry, "Glo - ry." The

an - gels cry "Ho - ly is the Lord!"
ser - aphs cry "Worth - y is the Lord!"
el - ders cry "A - men! It is so!"
peo - ple cry "Glo - ry to the Lord!"

79 When the Spirit Moves You

Words and Music by
Michael Fitzgerald

REFRAIN

When the Spir-it moves you, lord, you've got to____ move.____

_____ When the Spir-it moves you, lord, you've got to move.____

_____ When the Spir-it moves you, lord, good broth- er, you've got to

o- pen up your heart____ and lis- ten to Him.____ When the

Spir- it moves you, lord, you've got to move.____ *to verse*

VERSES

1. Now the Lord said to A- bra-ham,____ "Lead my peo-ple____ there,____ From the
2. Now the Lord said to Mos- es,_____ "Lead my peo-ple____ free,____ From the

land that you're set- tling____ to the land of Ca- naan."____ Now
land of the Pha- roah____ to the prom-ised____ land."____ Now

A- bra-ham said to the Lord,____ "An- y- thing You want to ask of me."
Mos- es said to the Lord,____ "An- y- thing You want to ask of me."

_____ When the Spir-it moves you, lord, you've got to move.____ *to refrain*
_____ When the Spir-it moves you, lord, you've got to move.____

3. Now lis- ten here, peo- ple___ to what I've got to___ say.___ When the

Lord speaks to us, we have to an- swer this way:___ We've got to

o- pen up our hearts to His love___ and hear His words of Truth.__

___ When the Spir-it moves you, lord, you've got to move.___ *to refrain*

Alabaré

REFRAIN

Unknown

A-la-ba - ré,__ a-la-ba - ré, a - la-ba-ré a mi Señ - or. A-la-ba-

ré,__ a-la-ba - ré, a - la-ba-ré a mi Señ - or.__ or.

VERSES

Juan vi -ó el nú - mer - o,__ de los red - i - mi-dos, y
John saw__ the num-ber__ of all__ those re - deemed, and

to - dos a -la - bab - an al Señ - or. U - nos o - ra - ban,__
all were sing-ing prais-es to the Lord. Thou-sands were pray-ing, ten

o - tros can - ta - ban, y to - dos a - la - bab - an al Señ - or.
thou-sands re - joic-ing, and all were sing-ing prais-es to the Lord.

No hay Dios tan grand - e co - mo Tu, No lo hay, no lo
There is no God as great as You, O Lord, there is none, there is

hay.__ No hay hay.__ No hay Dios que pued-e ha - cer las
none.__ There is no none.__ There is no God who does the might - y

co - sas co - mo las que ha - ces Tu.__ No hay Tu. No es con es-
won-ders that the Lord our God has done.__ There is no done. Nei-ther with an

pad - as, ni con e - jer -ci-tos, más con su San - to Es-pír - i-
ar - my, nor with their wea - pons, but by the Ho - ly Spir - it's

tu. No es con es tu. Y es -os mon - tes se mo-ver-
power. Nei-ther with an power. And e - ven moun-tains__ shall be

án. Yes-os mon-tes se mo-ver-án. Yes-os
moved. And e-ven moun-tains____ shall be moved. And e-ven

mon-tes se mo-ver-án. Más con su San-to Es-pir-i-tu.
moun-tains____ shall be moved. By the Ho-ly Spir-it's power.

to refrain

The following section may be sung several times, using the names of different countries.

Y Puer-to Ri-co se sal-va rá. Y Puer-to Ri-co se sal-va
And Puer-to Ri-co____ shall be saved. And Puer-to Ri-co____ shall be

rá. Y Puer-to Ri-co se sal-va rá. Más con su
saved. And Puer-to Ri-co____ shall be saved. By the

1.
San-to Es-pír-i-tu.
Ho-ly Spir-it's power.

Y (tam-bien) tu.
And (al-so) power.

2.

to refrain

202   **All of My Life**

Words and Music by
Germaine Kramlinger

REFRAIN

C   Em   Am   Em

All of__ my life   I will__ sing praise to my

Am   Em   Am

God. ____

VERSES

Am Em Am   G   Am   Em Am

1. For cre-a-tion, praise; For sal-va-tion__ praise; For all man-kind, praise.
2. For the Vir-gin, praise; For the saints and an-gels praise; For the Church,__ praise.

to refrain

Am   Em   Am   G   Am   Em   Am

3. To the Fa-ther, praise; To the Son, sing praise; To the Spir-it, praise.

to refrain

Alleluia, Sing to Jesus

203

Words by
William C. Dix

Music by
R. H. Prichard

Capo 3, Play D

1. Al - le - lu - ia! sing to Je - sus! His the scep - ter, His the throne;
2. Al - le - lu - ia! not as or - phans are we left in sor - row now;
3. Al - le - lu - ia! Bread of Heav - en, Thou on earth our food, our stay!

Al - le - lu - ia! His the tri - umph, His the vic - to - ry a - lone;
Al - le - lu - ia! He is near us, Faith be - lieves, nor ques - tions how:
Al - le - lu - ia! here the sin - ful flee to Thee from day to day;

Hark! the songs of peace - ful Zi - on thun - der like a might - y flood;
Though the cloud from sight re - ceived Him when the for - ty days were o'er,
In - ter - ces - sor, friend of sin - ners, earth's Re - deem - er, plead for me,

Je - sus out of eve - ry na - tion hath re - deemed us by His blood.
Shall our hearts for - get His prom - ise, "I am with you ev - er - more"?
Where the songs of all the sin - less sweep a - cross the crys - tal sea.

Amazing Grace

Words and Music by
John Newton

1. A - maz - ing grace, how sweet the sound that saved a wretch like me!
2. 'Twas grace that taught my heart to fear, and grace my fears re - lieved;
3. Through man - y dan - gers, toils, and snares, I have al - read - y come;
4. The Lord has prom - ised good to me, His word my hope se - cures;
5. And when this flesh and heart shall fail, and mor - tal life shall cease;
6. When we've been there ten thou - sand years, bright shin - ing as the sun,

I once was lost, but now am found, was blind, but now I see.
How pre - cious did that grace ap - pear the hour I first be - lieved!
'Tis grace has brought me safe thus far, and grace will lead me home.
He will my shield and por - tion be as long as life en - dures.
I shall pos - sess, with - in the veil, a life of joy and peace.
We've no less days to sing God's praise than when we'd first be - gun.

205

Amen, Our Hearts Cry

Based on Ex. 19:8

Words and Music by
John C. Blattner

G#7*
(F#7*)

REFRAIN
Capo 2, Play Bm

C#m(Bm)   A(G)   G#m(F#m)   C#m(Bm)

A - men, a - men our hearts cry, His word is

F#m G#m
(Em) (F#m) C#m(Bm)   A(G)   B(A)   C#m(Bm)

true. All that the Lord has said we will do.

206 As a Doe

Psalm 42 adapted by
Michael Fitzgerald

Music by
Michael Fitzgerald

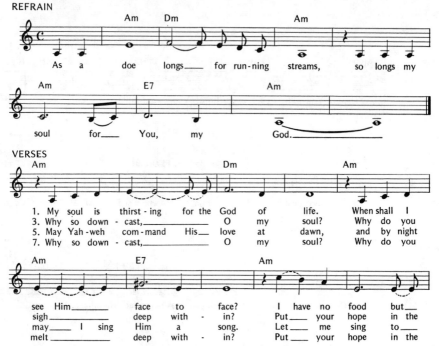

REFRAIN

As a doe longs____ for run-ning streams, so longs my soul for____ You, my God.____

VERSES

1. My soul is thirst-ing for the God of life. When shall I see Him____ face to face? I have no food but____
3. Why so down-cast,____ O my soul? Why do you sigh____ deep with-in? Put____ your hope in the
5. May Yah-weh com-mand His____ love at dawn, and by night may____ I sing Him a song. Let____ me sing to____
7. Why so down-cast,____ O my soul? Why do you melt____ deep with-in? Put____ your hope in the

tears day and night,___ and men say, "Where is your God?"___
God___ of life,___ I___ shall praise Him a - gain.___
God___ my ref - uge, "Why do you for - get___ me?"___
God___ of life, and I shall praise Him a - gain.___

2. I___ re - mem - ber___ and my soul melts with - in. I'm on my
4. When I find my soul___ down - cast with - in. I think of
6. Why must I walk___ op - pressed by the foe, all___ my
8. Glo - ry be___ to God the Fa - - ther, and___ to

way to the house___ of God, a - mong cries___ of
you, O Mount Zi - - on. Deep calls to deep as your
bones near - ly bro - ken with - in, as all day men___ say,
Je - sus the Lord,___ and to the Ho - ly

joy___ and praise. Place___ your trust___ in God.___
wa - ters roar. O - ver me all your waves pour.___
"Where is your God?" But I shall praise Him a - gain.___
Spir - - it. I will sing praise ev - er - more.___

to refrain

Blessed Be the Name

207

Words by
William H. Clark

Music by
Ralph E. Hudson

Bless- ed be the name, bless- ed be the name, bless- ed be the
Wor - thy to be praised, wor - thy to be praised, wor - thy to be
Je - sus is the name, Je - sus is the name, Je - sus is the

name of the Lord.___ Bless - ed be the name,
praised is the Lord.___ Wor - thy to be praised,
name of the Lord.___ Je - sus is the name,

bless- ed be the name, bless- ed be the name of the Lord.___
wor - thy to be praised, wor - thy to be praised is the Lord.___
Je - sus is the name, Je - sus is the name of the Lord.___

208   From Heaven the Lord Looks Down

Psalm 45:1

Words and Music by
Leo Nestor

VERSES

1. From heav'n the Lord looks down, up-on the chil-dren of men, to see if there be one who does good, and keeps the law in his heart.
2. Our hearts are rest-less for Thee, and rest-less al-ways shall be un-til they drink of the springs of Your love, and rise rest-less no more.
3. How love-ly is this place, the dwell-ing place of the Lord. My heart and soul have yearned and pined for God, the liv-ing God.

to refrain

REFRAIN

My heart o-ver-flows. I sing my ode to the King. My tongue flows like the pen of a scribe. I sing the praise of the Lord. Ooh.

Glorify Thy Name

209

Words and Music by
Donna Adkins

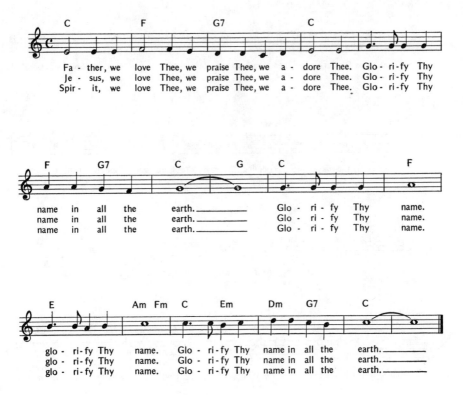

Fa - ther, we love Thee, we praise Thee, we a - dore Thee. Glo - ri-fy Thy
Je - sus, we love Thee, we praise Thee, we a - dore Thee. Glo - ri-fy Thy
Spir - it, we love Thee, we praise Thee, we a - dore Thee. Glo - ri-fy Thy

name in all the earth._____ Glo - ri - fy Thy name.
name in all the earth._____ Glo - ri - fy Thy name.
name in all the earth._____ Glo - ri - fy Thy name.

glo - ri-fy Thy name. Glo - ri-fy Thy name in all the earth._____
glo - ri-fy Thy name. Glo - ri-fy Thy name in all the earth._____
glo - ri-fy Thy name. Glo - ri-fy Thy name in all the earth._____

210 Grant to Us

Ez. 36:26 and Jer. 31:31-34 adapted by
Lucien Deiss, C.S.Sp.

Music by
Lucien Deiss, C.S.Sp.

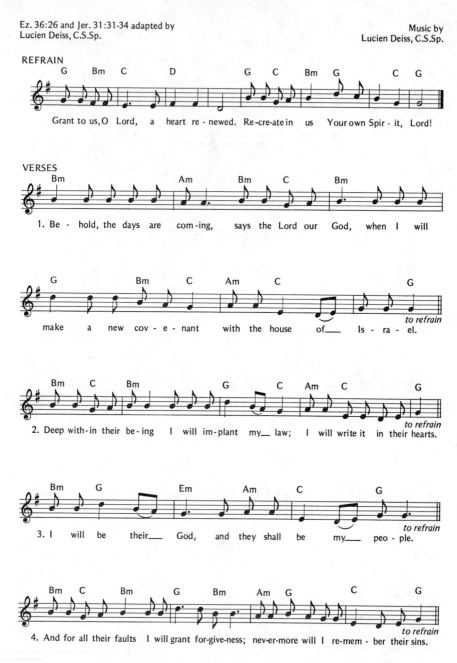

REFRAIN

Grant to us, O Lord, a heart re - newed. Re-cre-ate in us Your own Spir - it, Lord!

VERSES

1. Be - hold, the days are com -ing, says the Lord our God, when I will make a new cov - e - nant with the house of___ Is - ra - el.
to refrain

2. Deep with-in their be - ing I will im-plant my___ law; I will write it in their hearts.
to refrain

3. I will be their___ God, and they shall be my___ peo - ple.
to refrain

4. And for all their faults I will grant for-give-ness; nev-er-more will I re-mem - ber their sins.
to refrain

Hallelujah, My Father 211

Words and Music by
Tim Cullen

Hal - le - lu - jah, my Fa - ther, for giv - ing us Your Son, send - ing Him in - to the world to be giv - en up for man, Know - ing we would bruise Him and smite Him from the earth. Hal - le - lu - jah, my Fa - ther, in His death is my birth. Hal - le - lu - jah, my Fa - ther, in His life is my life.

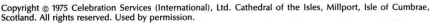

212   Hallelujah, Our God Reigns

Revelation 19:6-7

Words and Music by
Dale Garratt

Hal-le- lu-jah, for the Lord our God the Al- might - y____ reigns. Hal- le-

lu- jah, for the Lord, our God the Al- might - y____ reigns. Let us re-

joice and be glad and give the glo-ry un-to Him.____ Hal-le-

lu- jah, for the Lord our God the Al- might - y____ reigns.

Holy God, We Praise Thy Name   213

Ascribed to St. Nicetas
Tr. C. Walworth

Arranged by
Kalman Antos

Capo 3, Play D

1. Ho - ly God,___ we praise___ Thy___ Name! Lord of all___ we
2. Hark! the loud___ ce - les - tial___ hymn An - gel choirs___ a-

bow___ be - fore Thee; All on earth___ Thy scep - tre___ claim,
bove___ are rais - ing; Cher - u - bim___ and Ser - a - phim

All in heav'n___ a - bove___ a - dore Thee: In - fi - nite___ Thy
In un - ceas - ing cho - rus prais - ing; Fill___ the___ heav'ns___ with

vast___ do - main,___ Ev - er - last - ing is___ Thy reign. reign.
sweet___ ac - cord; Ho - ly, Ho - ly, Ho - ly Lord! Lord!

214 The Horse and Rider

Words anonymous
Exodus 15:1

Music by I. Miron and J. Grossman

I will sing un-to the Lord, for He has tri-umphed glo-rious-ly; the horse and rid-er thrown in-to the sea. sea. The Lord my God, my strength, my song, is now be-come my vic-to-ry. The ry. The Lord is God and I will praise Him, my fa-ther's God and I will ex-alt Him. The I will ex-alt Him.

This song is sometimes sung as a round. Numbers are included to indicate the three beginning points.

AFTER WILL JAMES

215   I Am the Resurrection

John 11:25-26

Words and Music by
Ray Repp

REFRAIN

I am the res-ur-rec-tion and the life; he who be-lieves in me will nev-er___ die. I am the res-ur-rec-tion and the life; he who be-lieves in me will live a new life. *to verse* live, will live a new life.___

VERSES

1. I have come to bring___ the___ truth; I have come___ to bring___ you___ life;___ if you be-lieve, then you shall___ live.___
2. In my word all men will come to know it is love___ which makes the spir-it grow.___ if you be-lieve, then you shall___ live.___
3. Keep in mind the things that I have said; re-mem-ber me in the break-ing of the bread.___ if you be-lieve, then you shall___ live.___

to refrain

I Hear a Sound

216

Words and Music by
Himmie Gustafson

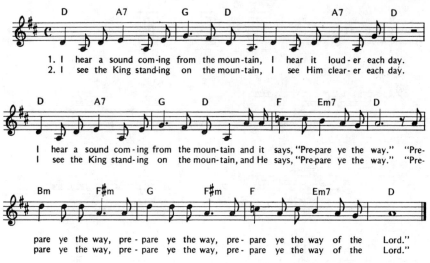

1. I hear a sound com-ing from the moun-tain, I hear it loud-er each day.
2. I see the King stand-ing on the moun-tain, I see Him clear-er each day.

I hear a sound com-ing from the moun-tain and it says, "Pre-pare ye the way." "Pre-
I see the King stand-ing on the moun-tain, and He says, "Pre-pare ye the way." "Pre-

pare ye the way, pre-pare ye the way, pre-pare ye the way of the Lord."
pare ye the way, pre-pare ye the way, pre-pare ye the way of the Lord."

217 Isaiah 60

Isaiah 60 adapted by
Donald Kopinski

Music by
Donald Kopinski

REFRAIN

A - rise, shine out, for your light has come. The glo - ry of
Yah-weh is ris-ing on you.___ Though night still cov-ers the earth, and
dark-ness the peo-ples,___ a - bove you, Yah-weh now ris - es; a - bove you His
glo-ry ap-pears; a - rise!___ *to verse* rise!___

VERSES

1. The na-tions come to Your light_ and kings to your dawn-ing bright-ness, sing-ing_ the
praise of Yah-weh,_ bring-ing gold_ and in-cense. Lift up your eyes and look a-round you;_
all are as-sem-bling and com-ing toward you. Your sons from far a-way,_ and your

daugh-ters be - ing ten-der-ly car-ried this day. _____

to refrain

2. They bring your sons from far a-way and their sil-ver and gold with them. For the name of

Yah-weh, your God, the Ho - ly One of Is - ra - el. ___ No more shall vio-lence be

heard in your coun-try, nor dev-a - sta-tion with - in your fron-tiers. You will call your

walls "Sal-va-tion," ___ and your gates "Praise." _____

to refrain

3. No more will the sun give you day-light, nor moon-light shine on you. ___ But

Yah-weh will be___ your e - ter-nal light; your God will be your splen-dor. Your sun will

set no more, ___ nor your moon wane, ____ but Yah-weh will be your e - ter-nal light

and your days of mourn-ing will pass from your sight. _____

to refrain

218 Jesus, I Love You

Words and Music by
Kathleen Thomerson

Capo 1, Play D

Verse lyrics:

1. Life is Your gift, I give my heart. Kneel and adore You and I know that
2. Now I have seen the love of God. He has poured out the Spirit of truth.
3. Love reaches out both near and far, and so we follow where You lead us.

Je-sus, I love You. Je-sus, I love You, love, love You, Je-sus, I love You. Take my life.

Je-sus, I fol-low, Je-sus, I fol-low,
Je-sus, I love You, Je-sus, I love You,

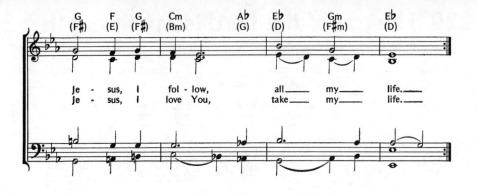

Je - sus, I fol - low, all____ my____ life.____
Je - sus, I love You, take____ my____ life.____

Joy Is the Flag

219

Unknown

Joy is the flag flown high from the cas-tle of my heart, from the

cas-tle of my heart, from the cas-tle of my heart. Joy is the flag flown high from the

cas-tle of my heart when the King is in res-i-dence there._ So let it fly in the sky, let the

whole world know, let the whole world know, let the whole world know. So let it

fly in the sky, let the whole world know that the King is in res-i-dence there.__

220 The Joy of the Lord Is My Strength

Refrain, verses 1 and 3 by Alliene Vale
Verse 2 unknown

Music by Alliene G. Vale

1. The joy___ of the Lord___ is my strength. The
2. If you___ want___ joy___ you must sing for it. If
3. Ah— ha ha ha ha ha ha ha ha ha ha. Ah—

joy___ of the Lord___ is my strength. The joy___ of the Lord___
you___ want___ joy___ you must shout for it. If you___ want___ joy___ you must
— ha ha ha ha ha ha ha ha ha ha. Ah— ha ha ha ha ha ha ha

is my strength. The joy___ of the Lord___ is my strength.
jump for it. The joy___ of the Lord___ is my strength.
ha ha ha. The joy___ of the Lord___ is my strength.

221 Keep in Mind

II Tim. 2:8-11 adapted by
Lucien Deiss, C.S.Sp.

Music by
Lucien Deiss, C.S.Sp.

REFRAIN

Keep in mind that Je - sus Christ has died for us and is ris - en from the

dead. He is our sav - ing Lord, He is joy for all a - ges.

VERSES

1. If we die with the Lord, we shall live with the Lord.
2. If we en - dure with the Lord, we shall reign with the Lord.

to refrain

3. In Him all our sor - row, in Him all our joy.
4. In Him hope of glo - ry, in Him all our love.
5. In Him our re - demp - tion, in Him all our grace.
6. In Him our sal - va - tion, in Him all our peace.

to refrain

Let Trumpets Sound

Words by
Michael Cockett

Music by
Kevin Mayhew

1-4. Ah _____ ah _____ ah

1. Where would we be with-out Christ, our Lord? We would be lost and
2. Where would we be with-out Christ, our Lord? We would be left to
3. Where would we be with-out Christ, our Lord? We would be cold and
4. Where would we be with-out Christ, our Lord? He is the Son who

walk-ing in dark-ness. He is the lan - tern that lights up the dark-ness, and
wan-der the des-ert. He is the bea - con that leads us to safe-ty, and
starv-ing and thirst-y. He is the bread that is food for the spir-it, and
saves all the na-tions. Through Christ the Son we are giv-en the Spir-it, and

he is the shep-herd that finds the right path. _____ So let the
he is the wa-ter that brings us new life. _____ So let the
he is the wine of the new cov-e-nant. _____ So let the
this is the Spir-it who brings us new life. _____ So let the

trum-pets sound to the glo-ry of God.__ He is my Lord, lov-ing and wise.
trum-pets sound to the glo-ry of God.__ He is my Lord, lov-ing and wise.
trum-pets sound to the glo-ry of God.__ He is my Lord, lov-ing and wise.
trum-pets sound to the glo-ry of God.__ He is my Lord, lov-ing and wise.

____ He is my Lord, _____ lov-ing and wise._____

223   Lift High the Banners of Love

Words and Music by
Rich Gillard

REFRAIN

Lift high the ban-ners of love, Hal-le - lu-jah. Sound the trum-pets of war.

Christ has got-ten us the vic-t'ry, Hal-le - lu-jah. Jer - i - cho must fall.

VERSES

1. The bod - y of Christ is an ar - my, fight - ing
2. Broth-ers, are you sure of your call - ing, will you fight for
3. We must stand in u - ni - ty, by the
4. Preach the Sav - ior cru - ci - fied, dead, but
5. In the name of God the Fa - ther, in the name of

pow - ers un - seen. Bring - ing the cap - tives to free - dom
Je - sus, the King? Are you pre - pared in this bat - tle
Spir - it made strong. Stand with Je - sus, our cap - tain,
ris - en a - gain. Come a-gainst the pow - ers of dark - ness
Je - sus His Son, And in the name of the Spir - it,

    in the name of Je - sus, our King.
    to lay down your lives for your friends?
    and fight till God's king - dom has come.
    in His glo - ri - ous name.
    we will fight till we are called home.

to refrain

Look Beyond

224

Based on John 6

Words and Music by
Darryl Ducote

REFRAIN
Capo 3, Play D

Look be-yond the bread you eat; See your Sav-ior and your Lord. Look be-yond the cup you drink; See his love poured out as blood.

VERSES

1. Give us a sign _____ that we might be-lieve in you. Our fa-thers bro't us man-na from the sky. _____
2. I am the bread _____ which from the heav-ens came; He who eats this bread will nev-er die. _____
3. The bread I give you _____ will be my ver-y flesh; My blood _____ will tru-ly be your drink. _____
4. This man speaks harsh-ly; _____ who can list-en to his word? We _____ shall no lon-ger fol-low him. _____
5. You, my dis-ci-ples, _____ will you _____ al-so leave? Lord, _____ to whom can we go? _____

last time only

See his love poured out as blood. _____

225 The Lord Is a Great and Mighty King

Words and Music by
Diane Davis

REFRAIN

The Lord is a great and might - y King, just and gen-tle with ev - er - y-

thing. So with hap -pi -ness___ we sing, and let His prais - es ring.

VERSES

1. We are His voice, we His song. Let us praise Him all day long. Al - le - lu - ia. *to refrain*

2. We are His Bod-y here on earth. From a-bove He gave us birth. Al - le - lu - ia. *to refrain*

3. For our Lord we will stand. sent by Him to eve -ry land. Al - le - lu - ia. *to refrain*

4. The Lord our God is ___ one: Fa-ther, Spir-it and the Son. Al - le - lu - ia. *to refrain*

One Thing I Ask For

226

Based on Psalm 27

Words and Music by
Ted Kennedy III

REFRAIN

One thing I ask for, that shall I seek: to dwell in the house of the
Lord._____ dwell in the house of the Lord._____ *to verse*

VERSES

1. All the days of my life, to be - hold___ the beau-ty of the Lord,
and to in - quire in His tem - ple.___ *to refrain*

2. You've___ said___ to me,___ "Seek ye my face."___
3. With___ all left be - hind, I seek on - ly God.___
4. I will wait for the Lord, and He gives me strength.___

My heart says, "Thy face do I seek!"___ *to refrain*
Teach___ me Your ways,___ O God.___ *to refrain*
For___ I have seen___ His good - ness!___ *to Coda*

One thing I ask for, that shall I seek: to dwell in the house of the
Lord.___ dwell in the house of the Lord.___ to
dwell in the house of the Lord.___

227

Our God Reigns

Words adapted from Isaiah 52:7 and
Isaiah 53 by Leonard E. Smith, Jr.

Music by
Leonard E. Smith, Jr.

Capo 1, Play A

How love-ly on the moun-tains are the feet of him who brings good news, good news, an-nounc-ing peace, pro-claim-ing news of hap-pi-ness— our God reigns, our God reigns. Our God reigns, our God reigns, our God reigns, our God reigns.

1. How lovely on the mountains are the feet of him
   Who brings good news, good news,
   Announcing peace, proclaiming news of happiness,
   Saying to Zion: Your God reigns.
   Chorus Your God reigns. . . 4x

2. He had no stately form, he had no majesty,
   That we should be drawn to him.
   He was despised and we took no account of him
   Yet now he reigns with the Most High.
   Chorus Now he reigns. . . 3x
   With the Most High.

3. It was our sin and guilt that bruised and wounded him,
   It was our sin that brought him down.
   When we like sheep had gone astray, our shepherd came
   And on his shoulders bore our shame.
   Chorus On his shoulders. . . 3x
   He bore our shame.

4. Meek as a lamb that's led out to the slaughter-house,
   Dumb as a sheep before it's shearer,
   His life ran down upon the ground like pouring rain
   That we might be born again.
   Chorus That we might be. . . 3x
   Born again.

5. Out from the tomb he came with grace and majesty,
   He is alive—he is alive.
   God loves us so—see here his hands, his feet, his side.
   Yes, we know—he is alive.
   Chorus He is alive. . . 4x

6. How lovely on the mountains are the feet of him
   Who brings good news, good news,
   Announcing peace, proclaiming news of happiness:
   Our God reigns—our God reigns.
   Chorus Our God reigns. . . 4x

Praise the Name of Jesus   228

Words and Music by
Roy Hicks, Jr.

Praise the name of Je - sus. Praise the name of Je - sus. He's my rock, He's my for-tress,

He's my de-liv-er-er, in Him will I trust. Praise the name of Je - sus.

229 The Prayer of St. Francis

Adapted by
Sebastian Temple

Music by
Sebastian Temple

1. Make me a chan-nel of Your peace.___ Where there is ha-tred, let me bring Your
2. Make me a chan-nel of Your peace.___ Where there's des-pair in life, let me bring

love.___ Where there is in - ju - ry, Your par - don, Lord,___ And
hope.___ Where there is dark-ness___ on - ly light,___ And

where there's doubt, true faith in You.___
where there's sad - ness ev - er joy.___ joy.___ Oh,

Mas-ter, grant that I may nev-er seek ___ so much to be con-soled as to con-

sole,___ to be un-der-stood as to un-der - stand,___ to be loved as to

love with all my soul.___ 3. Make me a chan-nel of Your

peace.___ It is in par-don- ing that we are par-doned,___ in giv-ing to all

men that we re - ceive,___ and in dy-ing that we're born to e-ter-nal life.

Priestly People

230

I Peter 2:9 adapted by
Lucien Deiss, C.S.Sp.

Music by
Lucien Deiss, C.S.Sp.

REFRAIN
Capo 2, Play G

Priest - ly peo - ple, King - ly peo - ple, Ho - ly peo - ple,

God's cho - sen peo - ple, Sing praise to the Lord.

VERSES

1. We sing to You, O Christ, be - lov - ed Son of the Fa - ther.
2. We sing to You, O Son, born of Mar - y the Vir - gin.
3. We sing to You, O bright - ness of splen - dor and glo - ry.
4. We sing to You, O light bring - ing men out of dark - ness.
5. We sing to You, Mes - si - ah fore - told by the proph - ets.

to refrain

We give You praise, O Wis - dom ev - er - last - ing, and Word of God.
We give You praise, Our Broth - er, born to heal us, Our sav - ing Lord.
We give You praise, O Morn - ing Star an - nounc - ing the com - ing day.
We give You praise, O guid - ing Light, who shows us the way to heaven.
We give You praise, O Son of Da - vid and Son of A - bra - ham.

6. We sing to You, Messiah, the hope of the people.
   We give You praise, O Christ, our Lord and King, humble, meek of heart.
7. We sing to You, The Way to the Father in heaven,
   We give You praise, The Way of Truth, and Way of all grace and light.
8. We sing to You, O Priest of the new dispensation,
   We give You praise, Our Peace, sealed by the blood of the Sacrifice.
9. We sing to You, O Lamb, put to death for the sinner,
   We give You praise, O Victim, immolated for all mankind.
10. We sing to You, The Tabernacle made by the Father,
    We give You praise, The Cornerstone and Savior of Israel.
11. We sing to You, The Shepherd who leads to the kingdom,
    We give You praise, Who gather all your sheep in the one true fold.
12. We sing to You, O Fount, overflowing with mercy.
    We give You praise, Who give us living waters to quench our thirst.
13. We sing to You, True Vine, planted by God our Father,
    We give You praise, O blessed Vine, whose branches bear fruit in love.
14. We sing to You, O Manna, which God gives his people.
    We give You praise, O living Bread, which comes down to us from heaven.
15. We sing to You, The Image of the Father eternal,
    We give You praise, O King of justice, Lord, and the King of peace.
16. We sing to You, The Firstborn of all God's creation,
    We give You praise, Salvation of your saints sleeping in the Lord.
17. We sing to You, O Lord, whom the Father exalted,
    We give You praise, In glory you are coming to judge all men.

231
Psalm 18

Psalm 18 adapted by
Jane Yankitis

Music by
Jane Yankitis

REFRAIN

last time to Coda

Yea, Thou dost light my lamp; the Lord my God light-ens my dark - ness.

to verse

VERSES

1. Yea, by Thee I can crush a troop; and by Thee I can leap a wall.

This God— His way is per-fect;— the prom-ise of the Lord proves true; He is my shield.—

to refrain

2. For who is God, but the Lord? And who is a rock ex-cept our God?— The

God who gird-ed me with strength, and made my way so ver - y safe.—

to refrain

3. He made my feet like hinds' feet— and set me se-cure up-on the heights.— He

trains my hands for war, so my arms can bend a bow of— bronze.—

to refrain

4. Thou hast giv-en me the shield of Thy sal - va-tion, and Thy right hand held me high, and Thy

help made me great. Thou didst give a wide place for my feet and they did not— slip.—

to refrain

5. The Lord lives, and bless-ed be my rock, and ex-alt-ed be the God of my sal-va-tion._ For
this_ I will ex - tol Thee, O Lord, a-mong the na-tions, and sing prais-es to Thy_ name. ____
to refrain

Yea, Thou dost light my lamp. ____

Psalm 150

232

Psalm 150 adapted by
Jan Vermulst

Music by
Jan Vermulst

REFRAIN
Capo 5, Play G

Al - le - lu - ia, al - le - lu - ia, al - le - lu - ia!

VERSES

1. Praise God in His ho - ly dwell - ing. ____
2. Praise Him with the blast of trum - pet. ____
3. Praise Him with re - sound - ing cym - bals, with
4. Praise God the al - might - y Fa - ther. ____

Praise Him on His might - y throne. Praise Him for His won - der - ful
Praise Him now with lyre and harp. Praise Him with the tim - brel and
cym - bals that ___ crash give praise. O, let ev - 'ry - thing that has
Praise Christ, His be - lov - ed Son. Give praise to the Spir - it of

deeds. Praise Him for His sov' - reign maj - es - ty! ____
dance. Praise Him with the sound of string and reed! ____
breath, let all liv-ing crea - tures praise the Lord! ____
love. For - ev - ver the tri - une God be praised! ____

233 ¡Resucitó, Resucitó!

Words and Music by
Kiko Argüello

REFRAIN
Capo 3, Play Em

iRe-su-ci-tó,___ re-su-ci-tó,___ re-su-ci-tó,___ a-le-lu-ya!___ a-le-lu-ya,___ a-le-lu-ya,___ a-le-lu-ya,___ a-le-lu-ya,___ re-su-ci-tó. tó, re-su-ci-tó.___

VERSES

1. La muer-te,___ ¿dón-de es-tá la muer-te?___ ¿Dón-de es-tá mi muer-te?___ ¿Dón-de su vic-to-ria?___

2. A-le-gri-a,___ a-le-gri-a her-man-os;___ que si hoy nos quer-e-mos,___ es por-que re-su-ci-tó.___

3. Si con Él mo-ri-mos,___ con Él vi-vi-mos,___ con Él can-ta-mos;___ iA-le-lu-ya!___

HE IS RISEN! ALLELUIA!
1. Death, where is death? Where is my death? Where is its victory?
2. Rejoice, brothers, for if today we love each other, it is because He is risen.
3. If we die with Him, we live with Him. We sing with Him, Alleluia!

Sing With All the Sons of Glory   234

Words by William J. Irons

Music by Ludwig van Beethoven
Arr. by Edward Hodges

1. Sing with all the sons of glory, Sing the res-ur-rec-tion song!
2. O what glo-ry, far ex-ceed-ing All that eye has yet per-ceived!
3. Life e-ter-nal! heaven re-joic-es: Je-sus lives who once was dead;
4. Life e-ter-nal! O what won-ders Crowd on faith; what joy un-known,

Death and sor-row, earth's dark sto-ry, To the for-mer days be-long.
Ho-liest hearts for a-ges plead-ing, Nev-er that full joy con-ceived.
Join, O man, the death-less voic-es; Child of God, lift up thy head!
When, a-midst earth's clos-ing thun-ders, Saints shall stand be-fore the throne!

All a-round the clouds are break-ing, Soon the storms of time shall cease;
God has prom-ised, Christ pre-pares it, There on high our wel-come waits;
Pa-triarchs from the dis-tant a-ges, Saints all long-ing for their heaven,
O to en-ter that bright por-tal, See that glow-ing fir-ma-ment,

In God's like-ness, man a-wak-ing, Knows the ev-er-last-ing peace.
Eve-ry hum-ble spir-it shares it, Christ has passed th'e-ter-nal gates.
Proph-ets, psalm-ists, seers, and sag-es All a-wait the glo-ry given.
Know, with Thee, O God im-mor-tal, "Je-sus Christ, whom Thou hast sent!" A-men.

235 Song of My People

Words and Music by
Juliet Pressel

A-bra-ham, A-bra-ham, where are you com-ing from, A-bra-ham?__ I'm com-ing from the land of the pa-gans, Lord.__ I'm com-ing to You,__ my__ God.

A-bra-ham, A-bra-ham,____ I will be your God.

Is-ra-el, Is-ra-el, why have you strayed from me, Is-ra-el?__ You say you don't need my__ guid-ing hand.__ You say you don't want my__ love.

Is-ra-el, Is-ra-el,____ I will be your God.

Gath-er 'round, lis-ten now to the words of a car-pen-ter__ Who walked the earth__ work-ing mir-a-cles,__ Who died for us__ on a cross.

C   Em   C   D   D7

"Take my hand,   walk with me.   I will be your   God."___

G   Em   C   D

Sons of men,   sons of men,   where are you com-ing from, sons of men?___ We're

Em   D   C   D

com-ing to You__ out of dark-ness, Lord.__ We're com-ing to You,__ our__ God

G   Em   C   D   G

Sons of men,   sons of light,_____ I will be your   God.

236 Song of Praise

Words and Music by
James Berlucchi

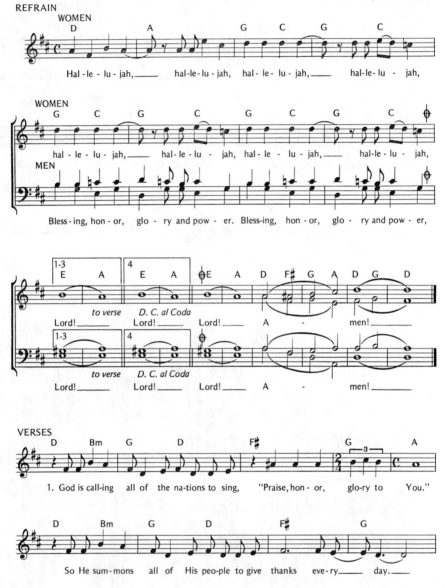

REFRAIN
WOMEN

Hal - le - lu - jah,___ hal - le - lu - jah, hal - le - lu - jah,___ hal-le-lu - jah,

WOMEN

hal - le - lu - jah,___ hal - le - lu - jah, hal - le - lu - jah,___ hal-le-lu - jah,

MEN

Bless - ing, hon - or, glo - ry and pow - er. Bless-ing, hon - or, glo - ry and pow - er,

Lord!___ Lord!___ Lord!___ A - men!

to verse   D. C. al Coda

Lord!___ Lord!___ Lord!___ A - men!

VERSES

1. God is call-ing all of the na-tions to sing, "Praise, hon - or, glo-ry to You."

So He sum-mons all of His peo-ple to give thanks ev-ery___ day.___

Thou-sands of voi-ces pro - claim, "God is light and He has shone on us." *to refrain*

2. We will see a horse with his ri-der, He is faith-ful and true to His word!

Crowned with glo-ry, eyes flam-ing fire, from His mouth is-sues a sword, the

might-y word of God. King of kings and Lord of lords is He! *to refrain*

3. We a-wait our heav-en-ly cit-y sing-ing, "Je-ru-sa - lem, God has named you."

He will make His home with His peo-ple, nev-er - more shall we cry, the

tears wiped from our eyes. All who thirst, drink deep from the well of life! *to refrain*

237 Song of Thanks

Words and Music by
Paul Quinlan

REFRAIN

Al - le - lu - ia, al - le - lu - ia, al - le - lu - ia, al - le - lu - ia, al-

- le - lu - ia, al - le - lu - ia, al - le - lu - ia, al - le - lu - ia. Al-

- le - lu - ia, al - le - lu - ia, al - le - lu - ia, al - le - lu - ia, al-

last time to Coda

- le - lu - ia, al - le - lu - ia, al - le - lu - ia, al - le - lu - ia. ___

to verse

- le - lu - ia, al - le - lu - ia, al - le - lu - ia, al - le - lu - ia! ___

VERSES

1. Sing a mer - ry song of thanks un - to the Lord.
2. In my troub - les all I go un - to the Lord.
3. All sur - round - ed when I strug - gled with my foe.
4. Loud re - joic - ing let there be in eve - ry home.
5. O - pen up___ your gates of glo - ry; let me through.
6. Blest are they___ who come___ in the name of God.

1. Through-out eve - ry age His mer - cy will en - dure. Is - ra - el___ will shout,
2. God is stand - ing by me; what man will I fear? To the Lord___ we ran,
3. Aw - ful rag - ing fire; they buzz like an - gry bees. God then heard___ my call,
4. God has come___ to help us, strong and ver - y brave. Now I will___ not die;
5. I'll give thanks___ to God who saved my lone - ly life. This day God___ has made;
6. God is Lord___ of all; His light on us has shone. Let us play___ a horn,

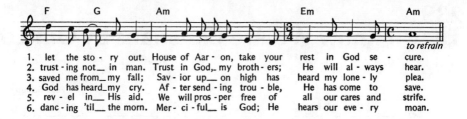

1. let the sto - ry out. House of Aar - on, take your rest in God se - cure.
2. trust-ing not__ in man. Trust in God,_ my broth - ers; He will al - ways hear.
3. saved me from__my fall; Sav - ior up__ on high has heard my lone - ly plea.
4. God has heard__my cry. Af - ter send - ing trou - ble, He has come to save.
5. rev - el in__ His aid. We will pros - per free of all our cares and strife.
6. danc - ing 'til__ the morn. Mer - ci - ful__ is God; He hears our eve - ry moan.

Therefore the Redeemed   238

Isaiah 51:11

Words and Music by
Ruth Lake

Capo 1, Play A

There-fore the re-deemed of the Lord shall re-turn and come with sing-ing__ un-to

Zi - on,__ and ev-er-last-ing__ joy shall be up-on their head. There-fore the re-

head. They shall ob - tain glad - ness and joy,__

__ and sor - row and mourn - ing__ shall flee a way.

There-fore the re-deemed of the Lord shall re-turn and come with sing-ing__ un-to

Zi - on,__ and ev-er-last-ing__ joy shall be up - on their head.__

239
They'll Know We Are Christians by Our Love

Words and Music by
Peter Scholtes

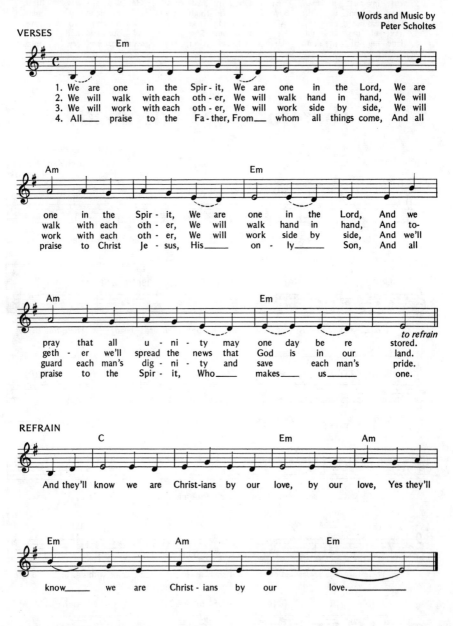

VERSES

1. We are one in the Spir-it, We are one in the Lord, We are
2. We will walk with each oth-er, We will walk hand in hand, We will
3. We will work with each oth-er, We will work side by side, We will
4. All praise to the Fa-ther, From whom all things come, And all

one in the Spir-it, We are one in the Lord, And we
walk with each oth-er, We will walk hand in hand, And to-
work with each oth-er, We will work side by side, And we'll
praise to Christ Je-sus, His on-ly Son, And all

to refrain

pray that all u-ni-ty may one day be re stored.
geth-er we'll spread the news that God is in our land.
guard each man's dig-ni-ty and save each man's pride.
praise to the Spir-it, Who makes us one.

REFRAIN

And they'll know we are Christ-ians by our love, by our love, Yes they'll

know we are Christ-ians by our love.

Thou Art Worthy

Revelation 4:11

Words and Music by
Pauline M. Mills

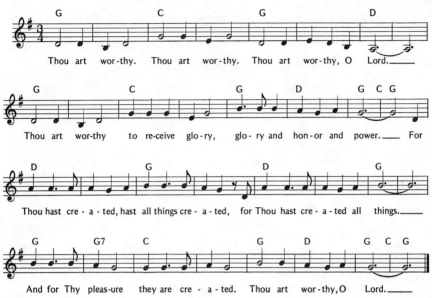

Thou art wor-thy. Thou art wor-thy. Thou art wor-thy, O Lord.

Thou art wor-thy to re-ceive glo-ry, glo-ry and hon-or and power. For

Thou hast cre-a-ted, hast all things cre-a-ted, for Thou hast cre-a-ted all things.

And for Thy pleas-ure they are cre-a-ted. Thou art wor-thy, O Lord.

Worthy Is the Lord

Words and Music by
Mark S. Kinzer

REFRAIN
Capo 2, Play D

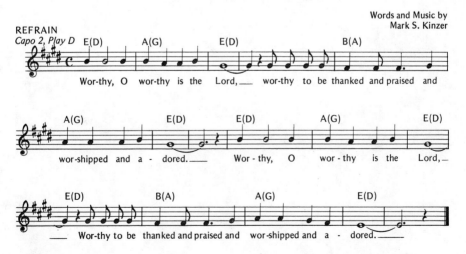

Wor-thy, O wor-thy is the Lord, worthy to be thanked and praised and

wor-shipped and a-dored. Wor-thy, O wor-thy is the Lord,

Wor-thy to be thanked and praised and wor-shipped and a-dored.

All Hail the Power of Jesus' Name 301

Words by
Edward Perronet
Alt. by John Rippon

'Coronation'

Music by
Oliver Holden

1. All hail the pow'r of Je - sus' name! Let an - gels pros - trate fall; Bring
2. Ye cho - sen seed of Is - rael's race, Ye ran-somed from the fall, Hail
3. Let ev - 'ry kin - dred, ev - 'ry tribe, On this ter - res - trial ball, To
4. O that with yon - der sa - cred throng We at His feet may fall! We'll

forth the roy - al di - a - dem, And crown Him Lord of__ all; Bring
Him who saves you by __ His - grace, And crown Him Lord of__ all; Hail
Him all maj - es - ty__ as - cribe, And crown Him Lord of__ all; To
join the ev - er - last - ing__ song, And crown Him Lord of__ all; We'll

forth the roy - al di - a - dem, And crown Him Lord__ of all!
Him who saves you by__His__grace, And crown Him Lord__ of all!
Him all maj - es - ty__ as - cribe, And crown Him Lord__ of all!
join the ev - er - last - ing__ song, And crown Him Lord__ of all!

302 All I Want

Phil. 3:8-10 adapted by
John Bagniewski

Music by
John Bagniewski

VERSE

1. I be-lieve that noth-ing can out-weigh the ad-van-tage of know-ing Je-sus Christ, the ad-van-tage of know-ing Christ Je-sus my Lord.

REFRAIN

All I want is to know Je-sus Christ and the pow-er of His ris-ing. All I want is to know my Lord and in Him to a-bide.

1-2. Ooh. *to verse*   3. Ooh.

VERSES

2. For Him I take the loss of eve-ry-thing, and I look on eve-ry-thing as naught, if on-ly I have Christ and a place in Him. *to refrain*

3. I'm no long-er try-ing on my own for per-fec-tion com-ing from the law; I want on-ly that which comes through my faith in Him. *to refrain*

Awake, O Israel

303

Several Old Testament passages
Adapted by Merla Watson

Music by
Merla Watson

1. A-wake, O Is - ra - el! Put off thy slum - ber, And the
2. For in the fur - nace of much af - flic - tion I have
3. Thou art my cho - sen, for I have sought thee, Thou art
4. O hal - le - lu - jah! O hal - le - lu - jah! Hal - le-

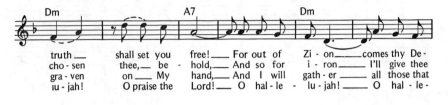

truth shall set you free! For out of Zi - on comes thy De -
cho - sen thee, be - hold, And so for i - ron I'll give thee
gra - ven on My hand, And I will gath - er all those that
lu - jah! O praise the Lord! O hal - le - lu - jah! O hal - le-

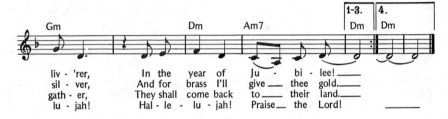

liv - 'rer, In the year of Ju - bi - lee!
sil - ver, And for brass I'll give thee gold.
gath - er, They shall come back to their land.
lu - jah! Hal - le - lu - jah! Praise the Lord!

304 Battle Hymn of the Republic

Words by
Julia W. Howe *Capo 1, Play A*

Music by
William Steffe

VERSES Bb (A)

1. Mine eyes have seen the glo-ry of the com-ing of the Lord; He is
2. I have seen Him in the watch-fires of a hun-dred cir-cling camps; They have
3. He has sound-ed forth the trum-pet that shall nev-er sound re-treat; He is
4. In the beau-ty of the lil-ies, Christ was born a-cross the sea, With a

Eb (D)　　　　　　　　　　　　　　　Bb (A)

tram-pling out the vin-tage where the grapes of wrath are stored; He hath
build-ed Him an al-tar in the eve-ning dews and damps; I can
sift-ing out the hearts of men be-fore His judg-ment seat; O be
glo-ry in His bos-om that trans-fig-ures you and me; As He

Bb (A)　　　　　　　　　　　　　　Cm (Bm)　F (E)　Bb (A)

loosed the fate-ful light-ning of His ter-ri-ble swift sword; His truth is march-ing on.
read His right-eous sen-tence by the dim and flar-ing lamps; His day is march-ing on.
swift, my soul, to an-swer Him! be ju-bi-lant, my feet! Our God is march-ing on.
died to make men ho-ly, let us live to make men free, While God is march-ing on.

REFRAIN
Bb (A)　　　　　　　　　　　　Eb (D)　　　　　　　　　Bb (A)

Glo-ry! glo-ry, hal-le-lu-jah! Glo-ry! glo-ry, hal-le-lu-jah!
Glo-ry! glo-ry, hal-le-lu-jah! Glo-ry! glo-ry, hal-le-lu-jah!
Glo-ry! glo-ry, hal-le-lu-jah! Glo-ry! glo-ry, hal-le-lu-jah!
Glo-ry! glo-ry, hal-le-lu-jah! Glo-ry! glo-ry, hal-le-lu-jah!

Bb (A)　　　　　　　　　　　　Cm (Bm)　F (E)　Bb (A)

Glo-ry! glo-ry, hal-le-lu-jah! His truth is march-ing on.
Glo-ry! glo-ry, hal-le-lu-jah! His day is march-ing on.
Glo-ry! glo-ry, hal-le-lu-jah! Our God is march-ing on.
Glo-ry! glo-ry, hal-le-lu-jah! While God is march-ing on.

Be Exalted, O God

305

Psalm 57:9-11

Capo 3, Play G

Music by
Brent Chambers

306 Behold

Based on Isaiah 12:2

Music by
Stuart Dauermann

Blessing and Glory

307

Revelation 7:12, 11:15, and 12:10

Capo 1, Play D

REFRAIN *(Sing twice at the beginning and the end.)*

Music by John Keating

308 Come and Worship

Words and Music by
A. Carter

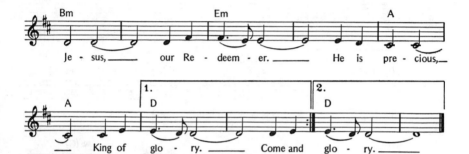

Come and wor - ship, ____ roy - al priest - hood. ____ Come and praise Him, ____ Ho - ly Na - tion. ____ Wor - ship Je - sus, ____ our Re - deem - er. ____ He is pre - cious, ____ King of glo - ry. ____ Come and glo - ry. ____

Come Back Singing

309

Psalm 126 adapted by
John Bagniewski

Music by
John Bagniewski

1. When Yah - weh brought the cap - tives home to Zi - on, it seemed like a dream to us at first. Then our mouths were filled with laugh - ter, laugh - ter, and on our lips a song. Come back sing - ing car - ry - ing the wheat, Hav - ing gone in weep - ing with the seeds. Now re - turn the har - vest with a song. Come back sing - ing car - ry - ing the wheat.

2. The pa - gans, e - ven they, be - gan to tell the mar - vels the Lord had done for us. And, in deed, He did for us great mar - vels. How o - ver - joyed we were.

3. Oh Yah - weh, bring all cap - tives back a - gain, like tor - rents up - on an ar - id land. Those who went to sow in tears and weep - ing will sing now as they reap.

3. wheat. Come back sing - ing car - ry - ing the wheat.

ritard

310 Come, Holy Spirit

Words and Music by
Mary Ackroyd

1. Come, Ho-ly Spir-it, and fill our hearts.
2. Thank you, Je-sus, for lov-ing us.
3. Thank you, Je-sus, for set-ting us free.
4. Thank you, Je-sus, for be-ing here.

Crown Him With Many Crowns 311

'Diademata'

Words by
Matthew Bridges

Music by
George J. Elvey

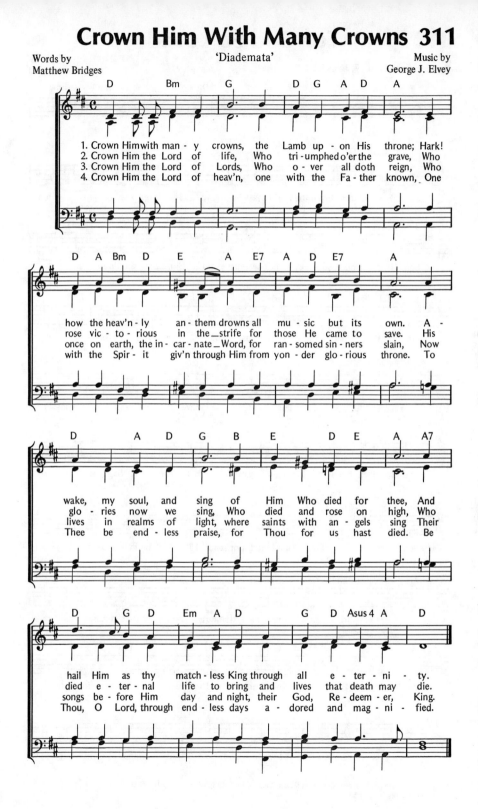

312 For God So Loved

Based on John 3:16-17, John 1:12

Music by
Stuart Dauermann

For God so loved the world that He gave— His on-ly be-got - ten

Son, That who-so-ev-er be-lieves in — Him— should not per -

ish, but have life ev-er-last-ing, have life ev-er-last-ing,

have life ev-er-last-ing, have life ev-er-last-ing. For

God so loved the world that He gave— His on-ly be-got - ten

Son. For God did not send His Son in-to the world

to bring con-dem-na-tion, But rath-er that, through the re -

ceiv-ing of Him, men might find true sal-va-tion, and *D.S al Coda*

He came in-to the world and He dwelt a-mong His own; But His

313 Glorious in Majesty

'Shibbolet Basadeh'

Words by
Jeff Cothran

Traditional Jewish Melody
Arr. by Jeff Cothran

Guitar, Piano, or Recorder
Introduction and Optional Interlude

(Triangle)

VERSES

Guitar chords are for rehearsal only

1. Glo - ri - ous   in ma - jes - ty,   ho - ly in   His prais - es,
2. Vic - to - ry   He won for us,   free - ing us   from dark - ness,
3. Breth - er - en,   we live in love,   liv - ing with   each oth - er,

(doo)

Je - sus,   our Sa - vior and our King.   Born a man   yet God of old,
dy - ing   and ris - ing from the dead.   Liv - ing with   the Fa - ther now,
glad - ly   we share each oth - er's pain.   Yet He will   not leave us so,

let us all   a - dore Him;   filled with   His Spir - it, let us   sing.
yet He is   a - mong us;   we are   the bo - dy, He the   head.
soon He is   re - turn - ing,   tak - ing   us back with Him to   reign.

REFRAIN

Liv - ing is to love Him, serv - ing Him to know His free - dom.

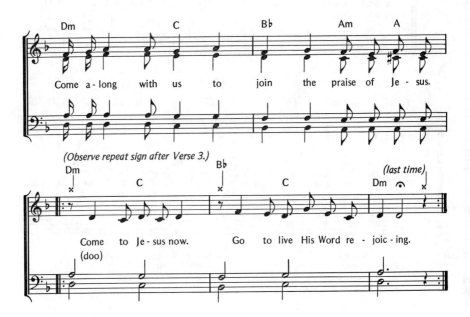

Come a - long with us to join the praise of Je - sus.

(Observe repeat sign after Verse 3.)

(last time)

Come to Je - sus now. Go to live His Word re - joic - ing.
(doo)

314 Glory Be to Jesus

Viva! Viva! Gesu (18th c. Italian hymn)
Translated by Edward Caswall, 1857.

Music by
Friedrich Filitz

Capo 5, Play C

1. Glo - ry be to Je - sus, Who in bit - ter pains
2. Grace and life e - ter - nal In that blood I find,
3. Blest through end - less a - ges Be the pre - cious stream

Poured for me the life - blood From his sa - cred veins!
Blest be his com - pas - sion In - fi - nite - ly kind!
Which from sin and sor - row Doth the world re - deem! A - men.

4. Oft as earth exulting
   Wafts its praise on high,
   Angel hosts, rejoicing,
   Make their glad reply.

5. Lift ye then your voices;
   Swell the mighty flood;
   Louder still and louder
   Praise the precious blood.   Amen.

God Is Raising an Army 315

Words and Music by
Mark Cowen

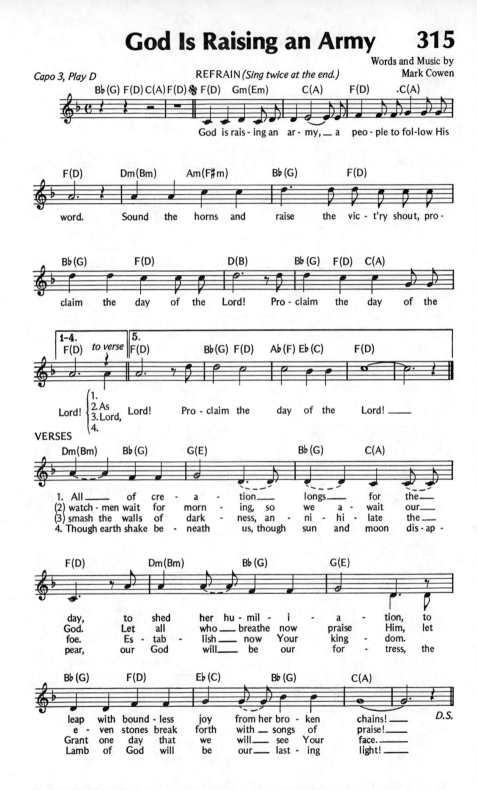

316 God, Make Us Your Family

Adapted from
Isaiah 35

Words and Music by
Tim Whipple

Capo 3, Play Dm

VERSE 1

1. The eyes of the blind shall be o-pened,___ the ears of the deaf shall hear.__ The chains of the lame will be bro-ken,___ streams will flow__ in des-erts of fear.___ Your

REFRAIN

king - dom come, your will__ be__ done, now that we have be-come your sons. Let the prayer of our hearts dai - ly__ be: God, make us your fam - i - ly. God, make us your fam - i - ly.___

to verse

2. The
3. The

VERSES 2 & 3

(2.) ran-somed of the Lord shall re - turn, ___ the is-lands will sing__ his songs at last. __
(3.) na - tions will see their shame,___ the one__ true God __ will be a-dored. __

___ The chaff from the wheat shall be burned, ___ his king-dom on earth, it shall
___ They turn from their for - tune and shame, ___ his ho - ly moun-tain shall

1.
come to pass.___ Your

D.S.

2. stored.___ Your

D.S. al Coda

God, make us your fam - i - ly.___

Optional refrains:

Laude, Lauda, Laude, Lauda. } repeat
Gloria, Emmanuel.

Alleluia, Alleluia } repeat
Glory to the living God.

Great and Wonderful

Based on Revelation 15:4

Music by
Stuart Dauermann

318 Hail to the Lord's Anointed

Based on Psalm 72
James Montgomery 1771-1854

'Yeldall'

Music by
Betty Pulkingham

1. Hail to the Lord's a-noint-ed, Great Da-vid's great-er Son!_ Hail in the time ap-point-ed, His reign on earth be-gun! _____ He comes to break op-pres-sion, To set the cap-tive_ free; _____ To take a-way trans-gres-sion, And rule_ _____ in e-qui-ty.

2. He shall come down like show-ers, Up-on the fruit-ful earth,_ And love, joy, hope, like flow-ers, Spring in his path to birth: _____ Be-fore him on the moun-tains Shall peace, the her-ald,_ go; _____ And right-eous-ness in foun-tains From hill_ _____ to val-ley flow.

3. Kings shall bow down be-fore_ him, And gold and in-cense bring;_ All na-tions shall a-dore_ him, His praise all peo-ple sing; _____ For he shall have do-min-ion O'er eve-ry sea_ and _ shore; _____ His king-dom still in-creas-ing, A king-dom_ His for ev-er_ _____ more.

4. O'er eve-ry foe vic-tor-i-ous, He on his throne shall rest;_ From age to age more glo-ri-ous, All bless-ing and all-blest: _____ The tide of time shall nev-er His cov-e-nant_ re-move; _____ His name shall stand for-ev-er, His change-less name_ of_ love.

Hevenu Shalom Aleikhem

319

Traditional

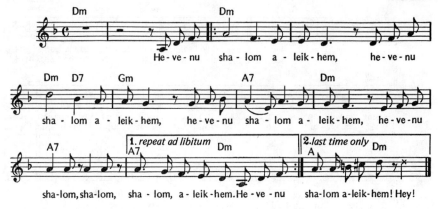

He - ve - nu sha - lom a - leik - hem, he - ve - nu
sha - lom a - leik - hem, he - ve - nu sha - lom a - leik - hem, he - ve - nu
sha - lom, sha - lom, sha - lom, a - leik - hem. He - ve - nu sha - lom a - leik - hem! Hey!

We bring you peace.

Hiney Mah Tov

320

Psalm 133:1

Traditional

Hin - ey mah tov u
hold, how good and

mah na - im, shev - et a - chim gam yach - ad. Hin -
pleas - ant it is for breth - ren to dwell to - geth - er. Be -

ey mah tov u - mah na - im, shev - et a - chim gam
Hold, how good and pleas - ant it is for breth - ren to dwell to -

yach - ad. Hin - ey mah tov, hin - ey mah tov. La la
geth - er. In u - ni - ty, to dwell in u - ni - ty. La la

la, la la la la la la la. Hin - ey mah tov, hin - ey mah
la, la la la la la la la. In u - ni - ty, to dwell in u - ni

tov. La la la, la la la la la la la. Be -
ty. La la la, la la la la la la la.

321 I Will Sing, I Will Sing

Words and Music by
Max Dyer

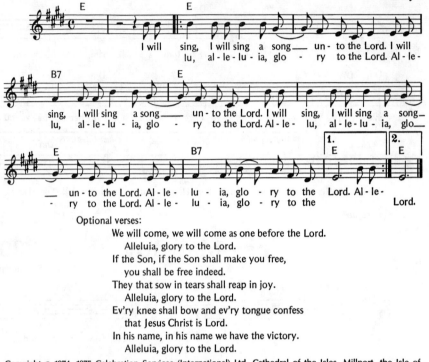

I will sing, I will sing a song — un-to the Lord. I will
lu, al-le-lu-ia, glo - ry to the Lord. Al-le-

sing, I will sing a song — un-to the Lord. I will sing, I will sing a song —
lu, al-le-lu-ia, glo - ry to the Lord. Al-le - lu, al-le-lu-ia, glo —

— un-to the Lord. Al-le - lu-ia, glo - ry to the Lord. Al-le-
- ry to the Lord. Al-le - lu-ia, glo - ry to the Lord.

1. Lord.
2. Lord.

Optional verses:

We will come, we will come as one before the Lord.
  Alleluia, glory to the Lord.
If the Son, if the Son shall make you free,
  you shall be free indeed.
They that sow in tears shall reap in joy.
  Alleluia, glory to the Lord.
Ev'ry knee shall bow and ev'ry tongue confess
  that Jesus Christ is Lord.
In his name, in his name we have the victory.
  Alleluia, glory to the Lord.

322 Isaiah 43

Isaiah 43
Adapted by Cathy Zawacki

Music by
Cathy Zawacki

REFRAIN A

Yah-weh, You have cre - a-ted me. — You have called me by name, —

1,5. and I — am — Yours. — *to Refrain B*
2,3,4. Yours. — *to verse 2, 3, 4*

REFRAIN B

For-ev-er — I will sing of Your good-ness. — I will walk now in free - dom. —

323 Let us Come and Bow Down

Words and Music by
James Berlucchi

REFRAIN

Let us come and bow down be-fore__ our God and King:__ "My glo - ry and the lift - er of__ my head."__ Let us come and sac - ri - fice eve-ry-thing__ to the One who raised_Christ Je - sus from the dead. _

1,4. — **2,3.** Let us _to verse_ **5.**

VERSES

1. Let us not__ lose heart in run - ning the race. __

Let us look to Je - sus the found - er of our faith.

Let us lift__ our droop - ing hands and strength - en our knees__

to fol - low the Lord, our God, the King of Kings. __ Let us

2. For who is like the Lord, our sav - ior?

Search the heav - ens, search the earth; there is none like Him.

Ho - ly, Ho - ly Lord God Al - might - y,

all cre - a - tion is full of Your glo - ry. Let us

Verses may be improvised, using the two above as models.

324 Let Us Give Thanks

Adapted from
Luke 10: 17, John 10: 10

Words and Music by
Brian Howard

REFRAIN

Let us give thanks that our names are writ-ten,

Let us give thanks that our names are writ-ten,

Writ-ten in the book of life and in-scribed up-on His palms,

Writ-ten in the book of life and in-scribed up-on His palms.

VERSES

1. Re-joice not that dev-ils flee in His name.

Re-joice not in the pow-er that He gave.

For He came to break the bonds of sin.

325   Let Us Sing

Words and Music by
Roger L. Holtz

REFRAIN *(Sing twice at the beginning and the end.)*

Let us sing to the Lord with our whole heart. Let us sing to the Lord with our whole strength. Let us offer the Lord a sacrifice of praise, for He has done marvelous things. *to verse* things.

VERSES

1. We will no longer be afraid. We will wear the whole armor of our God. We will march on to war beneath the banner of the Lord and be victorious evermore. *D.S.* Let us

It is customary to improvise verses for this song, using the chord progression of the printed verse.

Lion of Judah

Words and Music by
Ted Sandquist

1., 4. Li - on of Ju - dah, on the throne,__
2. Li - on of Ju - dah, come to earth,__
3. Li - on of Ju - dah, come a - gain,__

I shout Your name.__ Let it be known that You are
I want to thank __ You for Your birth. For the
Take up Your throne,__ Je - ru - sa - lem. Bring re -

King of Kings,__ You are____ the Prince __ of Peace. May Your
liv - ing Word,__ For Your____ death on ___ the tree, For Your
lease to this earth, and the con - sum - ma - tion of Your

King - dom's reign ____ nev - er cease! Hail to __ the King! ____ Hail to __ the
res - ur - rec - tion vic - to - ry! Hal - le - lu - jah! ____ Hal - le - lu -
king - dom's reign, ____ let __ it come! Mar - a - na - tha! ____ Mar - a - na -

King! ____ ____ Hail to __ the King! ____ Hail to __ the
jah! ____
tha! ____

King! You are my King! ____

327 The Lord Is Blessing Me Right Now

Capo 1, Play G

Unknown

The Lord is bless-ing me — right now, right now. The
Lord is bless-ing me — right now, right now. You may not be
a-ble to see — all the Lord has done for me, — but the Lord — is
bless-ing me — right now, right now. The bless-ing me, but the Lord — is
bless-ing me, but the Lord — is bless-ing me — right now, right now.

1. *repeat ad libitum*
2. *last time only*

Copyright unknown.

328   The Magnificat

Luke 1:46-55
Adapted by Charles Christmas

Music by
Charles Christmas

REFRAIN

My soul ___ mag - ni - fies the
My soul mag - ni - fies the
Lord, ___ and my spir - it ___ re - joic - es ___ in
Lord. ___ My spir - it re - joic - es in
God ___ my Sav - ior. ___ He Sav - ior. ___ My

1-3. to verse
4. to Coda

1. For
2. He
3. The

God ___ my Sav - ior. ___ He Sav - ior.

1. For
2. He
3. The

VERSES

(1) He Who is might-y has done great things, and ho-ly is His name. From age to age His mer-cy is on those who fear Him. He fills the hun-gry with good things; He helps those who serve Him. My

(2) scat-ters the proud and He lifts up the low-ly. He has shown strength with His arm. For the Word be-came flesh and He dwelt a-mong us. No one has seen the Fa-ther, but the Son has made Him known. My

(3) words of the Lord are Spir-it and life. Bless-ed are the peo-ple who hear them and keep them. When God speaks His word, let it be ful-filled in me. For with the Lord, noth-ing is im-pos-si-ble. My

spir-it re-joic-es in Je-sus, my Sav-ior.

My spir-it re-joic-es in Je-sus, my Sav-ior.

329 My Glory and the Lifter of My Head

Adapted from
Psalm 3:3-4

Words and Music by
Mae McAlister

My glo-ry and the lift-er of my head, my glo-ry and the lift-er of my head! And Thou, O Lord, art a shield to me,___ my glo-ry and the lift-er of my head! I cried un-to the Lord with my voice!___ I cried un-to the Lord with my voice! I cried un-to the Lord with my voice,___ and He heard me out of His ho-ly hill!___ My glo-ry and the lift-er of my head, my glo-ry and the lift-er of my head!___ And Thou, O Lord, art a shield to me,___ my glo-ry and the lift-er of my head! My head!

Now Let Us Sing

'Let Us Sing Till the Power of the Lord Come Down'

330

Words and Music by
A.B. Windom

331 Once No People

Based on I Peter 2:9-10
Maggie Durran

Music by
Betty Pulkingham

REFRAIN

For we are a cho-sen race, a roy-al priest-hood, ho-ly na-tion. Once no peo-ple, now God's peo-ple, pro-claim-ing His mar-vel-ous light.

VERSES

1. Sing the songs of faith-ful Zi-on, we are the stars and the grains of sand. Through our faith we are made glo-ri-ous, we are sons of A-bra-ham.

2. Dance the steps of joy-ful Zi-on, cym-bals, harps, and tam-bour-ines. Blow the trum-pet, sound the glo-ry, in the pres-ence of the Lord.

3. Taste the fruit of peace-ful val-leys, sip of the wine and eat the bread. Know the shep-herd who is guid-ing, the Lord, the Lamb of God.

4. We will serve through trib-u-la-tion, we will fol-low to the cross. Know the death and pain of suf-fer-ing, God wipes the tears from our eyes.

332 Proclaim His Marvelous Deeds

Psalm 96 adapted by
Donald E. Fishel

Music by
Donald E. Fishel

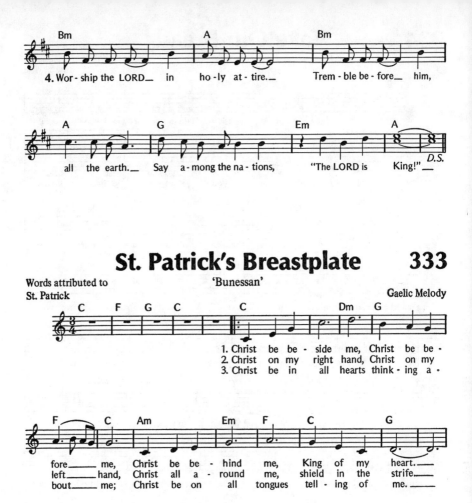

4. Wor-ship the LORD__ in ho-ly at-tire.__ Trem-ble be-fore__ him, all the earth.__ Say a-mong the na-tions, "The LORD is King!"__ *D.S.*

St. Patrick's Breastplate   333

Words attributed to
St. Patrick

'Bunessan'

Gaelic Melody

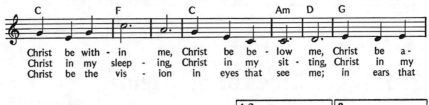

1. Christ be be-side me, Christ be be-
2. Christ on my right hand, Christ on my
3. Christ be in all hearts think-ing a-

fore__ me, Christ be be-hind me, King of my heart.__
left__ hand, Christ all a-round me, shield in the strife.__
bout__ me; Christ be on all tongues tell-ing of me.__

Christ be with-in me, Christ be be-low me, Christ be a-
Christ in my sleep-ing, Christ in my sit-ting, Christ in my
Christ be the vis-ion in eyes that see me; in ears that

1,2.
bove me, nev-er to part.__
ris-ing, light of my life.__
hear me, Christ ev-er

3.
be.__

334 Take Our Bread

Words and music by
Joseph Wise

REFRAIN

Take our bread, we ask you; take our hearts, we love you. Take our lives, oh Fa-ther; we are yours, we are yours. yours.

VERSES

1. Yours as we stand at the ta-ble you set; Yours as we eat the bread our hearts can't for-get. We are the sign of your life with us yet, we are yours, we are yours. Take our

2. Your ho-ly peo-ple stand-ing washed in your blood, Spir-it-filled yet hun-gry we a-wait your food. We are poor, but we've brought our-selves the best we could; we are yours, we are yours. Take our

335 Trees of the Field

Isaiah 55:12 adapted by
Steffi Geiser-Rubin

Music by
Stuart Dauermann

You shall go out with joy___ and be led forth with peace.___ The moun-tains and the hills will break forth be-

336 Unto the House of the Lord

Psalm 122 adapted by
John Bagniewski

Capo 3, Play D

Music by
John Bagniewski

REFRAIN

I re-joiced when they said to me, "Let us go____ un-to the house of the Lord,"

____ stand-ing there, O Je-ru-sa-lem,____ in your gates____

____ un-to the house of the Lord. ____

VERSES

1. Look up-on Je-ru - sa-lem,____ the cit-y now re-stored.____
2. As He or-dered Is - ra-el,____ they come to praise His name____
3. Pray for peace, Je-ru - sa-lem, ____ pros-per-i - ty at home,____
4. Since we are God's peo - ple, ____ I say, "Peace be to you!" ____

Here the tribes of Yah - weh come ____ as one un - to the Lord. ____ *D.S.*
Here where courts of jus - tice, ____ the courts of Da - vid, reign. ____
Peace in - side your cit - y walls ____ that comes from God a - lone. ____
May the God who dwells ____ in us ____ your hap - pi - ness re - new. ____

337 We Will Sing to the Lord Our God

Words and Music by
Richard Gullen

We will

sing to the Lord____ our God, ____ might-y and splen-did is He! ____

338 You Are Near

Psalm 139 adapted by
Dan Schutte, S.J.

Music by
Dan Schutte S.J.

REFRAIN

Yah - weh, I know you are near,____ stand - ing al - ways at my side.____ You guard me from the foe, and you lead me in ways ev - er - last - ing.____ last - ing.____

VERSES

1. Lord, you have searched my heart, and you know when I sit and when I stand. Your__ hand is up - on me pro - tect - ing me from death, keep - ing me from harm.____

2. Where can I run from your love? If I climb to the heav - ens you are there; if I fly to the sun - rise or sail be - yond the sea,

Am7 *slowing* **Am7/G** **D/F♯** *ritard*

still I'd find you there.___ *D.S.*

G **C9** **D** **Em** **Am**

3. You know my heart and its ways, you who formed me be-fore I was

Bm **Em** **Am** **Bm**

born in the se - cret of dark - ness be - fore I saw the sun

Am7 *slowing* **Am7/G** **D/F♯** *ritard*

in my moth - er's womb.___ *D.S.*

G **C9** **D** **Em** **Am**

4. Mar - vel - ous to me are your works; how pro - found are your thoughts, my ___

Bm **Em** **Am** **Bm**

Lord. E - ven if I could count them, they num - ber as the stars,

Am7 *slowing* **Am7/G** **D/F♯**

you would still be there.___ *D.S.*

339 You Shall Be My Witnesses

with spirit · REFRAIN

Words and Music by
Sr. Mary Mc Cooey, H.R.S.

You___ shall be my wit-ness-es un - to the ends of the earth, wit - ness - ing to my truth and to my love.___

VERSES

1. If you fol - low___ in my foot - steps,___ you shall be my wit - ness, if you take___ up___ your___ cross and fol - low me___ and do not___ be a - fraid,___ but be - lieve___ in___ me.

2. If you a - bide___ in___ me___ you shall be my wit - ness, for with me in___ you, you___ will bear fruit in plen - ty, a___ fruit___ that___ will re - main,___ a___ fruit___ that will last.

3. If you love___ one an - oth - er, ___ you shall be my wit - ness, for then eve - ry - one___ will___ know that you are mine, ___ when you love___ one an - oth - er in ___ truth, ___ as___ I have loved___ you.

4. If you are filled ___ with the Spir - it, ___ you shall be my wit - ness. What to say will be giv - en you, so ___ do not be a - fraid, ___ for___ he who is the Spir - it ___ of your Fa - ther ___ will ___ speak in you.

1-3. · 4. D.S. al Coda

DESCANT

To the

MELODY

You____ shall be my wit-ness-es   un - to the ends,   the

HARMONY

You____ shall be my wit-ness-es   to the

ends   of   the   earth.____

ends   of   the   earth.____

ends____   of   the   earth.____

Ascribe to the Lord

401

Words adapted from Psalm 29 by
James Berlucchi

Music by
James Berlucchi

VERSE 1

WOMEN: 1. A - scribe to the Lord,___ O___ heav'n - ly beings, a - scribe to him glo - ry___ and strength. O come a - scribe to the Lord ___ the glo-ry of his name, and wor-ship him___ in ho-ly___ ar - ray.

MEN: The voice of God is up - on man-y wa - ters.___ The God of glo - ry___ thun - der-ing forth. The voice of God, full of maj-es-ty___ and pow - er.___

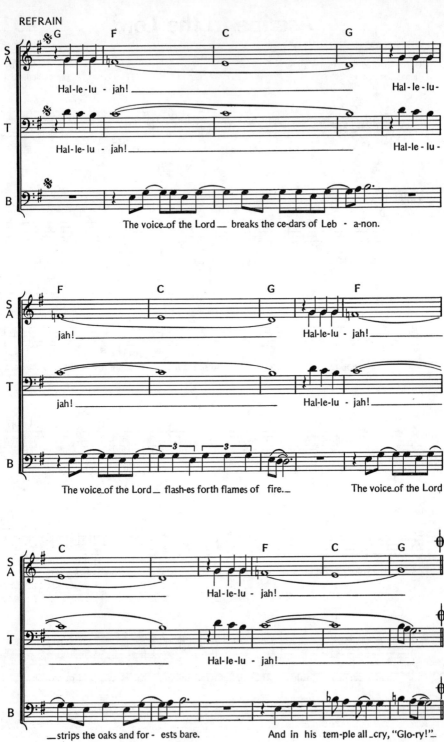

402 Be With Me, Lord

Psalm 91

Music by
Donald E. Fishel

REFRAIN

Am9   G9   Am9

Be with me, Lord,___

Am9   G9   1. Am

___ when I am in trou - ble.____ Be with me, Lord.____ Be

2-4. Am   to verse 5. Am   to verse 6. Am

Lord.____   1.   Lord.____   4. Be-cause he   Lord.____
     2. No
     3. Up -

VERSES

Am   D

1. You who dwell in the shel - ter, in the shel - ter of the Most_High, who a -

G   C   Em

bide__ in the shad-ow of the Al - might-y,_____ Say to the LORD,__ "My

Em   Am   G   D.S.

ref - uge__ and my for - tress, my__ God, in whom I trust."___ Be

D

e - vil shall be - fall _you, no__ e - vil shall be - fall _you, nor shall af -

403 Blessed Be the Lord, My Rock

Psalm 144 adapted by
Mark B. Foster

Music by
Mark B. Foster

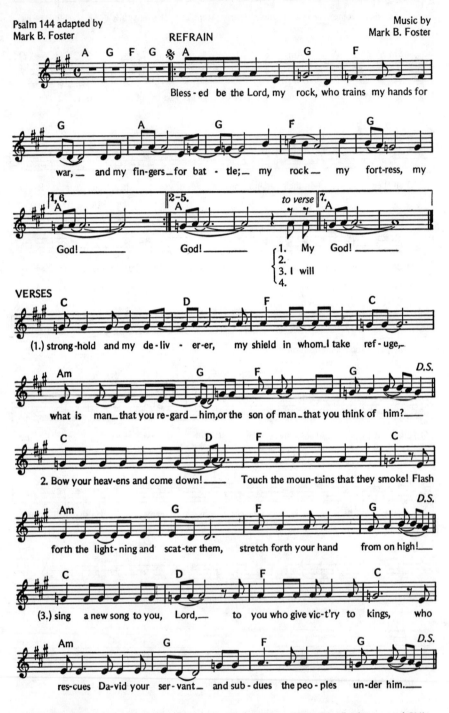

REFRAIN

Bless-ed be the Lord, my rock, who trains my hands for war, __ and my fin-gers __ for bat - tle; __ my rock __ my fort-ress, my

God! __ God! __ 1. My God! __

VERSES

(1.) strong-hold and my de-liv - er-er, my shield in whom I take ref - uge, __ what is man __ that you re-gard __ him, or the son of man __ that you think of him? __

2. Bow your heav-ens and come down! __ Touch the moun-tains that they smoke! Flash forth the light-ning and scat-ter them, stretch forth your hand from on high! __

(3.) sing a new song to you, Lord, __ to you who give vic-t'ry to kings, who res-cues Da-vid your ser-vant __ and sub-dues the peo-ples un-der him. __

4. May our sons in their youth_ be like plants full grown.

Hap-py the peo-ple with such bless-ings,_ the peo-ple whose God is the Lord!_

The Celebration Song

404

Psalm 22:3,25
Adapted by Brent Chambers

Music by
Brent Chambers

In the pres-ence of Your peo-ple
Lai lai lai lai lai lai lai lai,

I will praise Your name, for a - lone You are ho - ly, en -
lai lai lai lai lai. Lai lai lai lai lai lai lai lai

throned on the prais-es of Is - ra - el. Let us cel - e-brate Your good-ness
lai lai lai lai lai lai lai lai lai. Lai lai lai lai lai lai lai lai,

and Your stead - fast love. May Your name be ex - alt - ed
lai lai lai lai lai. Lai lai lai lai lai lai lai

here on _ earth and in heav'n a - bove. lai lai_ lai lai lai lai lai lai.

405 Create in Me

Psalm 51 adapted by
George Misulia

Music by
George Misulia

406 The Dwelling of God Is Among You Today

Revelation 21 adapted by
Don Austin

Music by
Don Austin

And then I heard a loud voice say,

Be-hold, the dwel-ling of God is a-mong you to-day!

And He shall wipe a-way your tears; there'll be no

mourn-ing, or cry-ing, or pain,— or death an-y more!

Hal - le - lu - jah! Hal - le - lu - jah!___

___ For the Lord God Al - might - y, Om - ni - po - tent

reigns! Our might - y___ God! Our ris - en ___

Lord!_____ All the glo - ry, and hon - or, and

pow - er___ are Yours ev - er - more! more!_____

Father, Make Us One

John 17:21
Psalm 133:1,3

Words and Music by
Rick Ridings

408

For All the Saints

'Sine Nomine'

William W. How, 1823-1897

Ralph Vaughan Williams, 1872-1958

unison

1. For all the saints who from their la - bors rest, Who
2. Thou wast their rock, their for - tress, and their might;___
3. O may thy sol - diers, faith - ful, true, and bold,___
4. O blest com - mu - nion, fel - low - ship di - vine!___
5. And when the strife is fierce, the war - fare long,___
6. The gold - en eve - ning bright - ens in the west;___
7. But lo! there breaks a yet more glo - rious day; The
8. From earth's wide bounds, from o - cean's far - thest coast, Through

thee___ by faith be - fore the world con - fessed, Thy
Thou, Lord, their cap - tain in the well - fought fight;___
Fight as the saints who no - bly fought of old, And
We fee - bly strug - gle, they in glo - ry shine; Yet
Steals on the ear the dis - tant tri - umph song, And
Soon, soon to faith - ful war - riors com - eth rest;___
saints___ tri - umph - ant rise in bright ar - ray; The
gates___ of pearl streams in the count - less host,___

Music from *The English Hymnal* by permission of Oxford University Press, Ely House, 37 Dover Street, London
W1X 4AH, England.

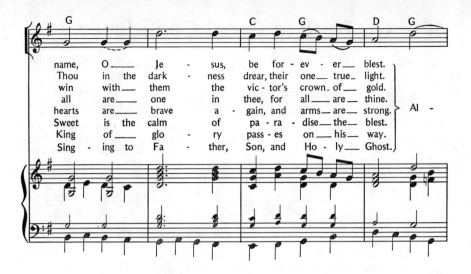

name, O____ Je - sus, be for - ev - er___ blest.
Thou in the dark - ness drear, their one__ true_ light.
win with__ them the vic - tor's crown_ of__ gold.
all are__ one in thee, for all__ are__ thine.
hearts are__ brave a - gain, and arms__ are__ strong. Al -
Sweet is the calm of pa - ra - dise_ the_ blest.
King of__ glo - ry pass - es on __ his_ way.
Sing - ing to Fa - ther, Son, and Ho - ly__ Ghost.

- le - lu - ia, Al - le - lu - ia! A - men.

409 Go Forth in Great Confidence

Words and Music by
Stacy Whitfield

VERSES

1. Sol - diers pre - par - ing for war, a-
2. Who is the cap-tain of your ar - my?
3. Robed in the strength of your God and
4. God a - lone is your Rock, a
5. Know, too, the love of your breth-ren,

noint - ed with pow - er by your King, Now gird up the
Let Him ride out a - head of you, Pre - par - ing the
clothed in the ar - mor He pro-vides, Is there one to
For - tress for you in time of need, And He is the
let it en - cour - age you, For though you go

loins of your minds that you may be ful - ly pre-pared.
path you are to take, then rid - ing a - long - side of you.
o - ver-come you? No, you shall not be dis-turbed at all. } Go
source of your strength; with - out Him you could not suc-ceed.
forth from their midst, still you re - main one with them.

REFRAIN

forth now in great con-fi-dence for you shall not be put down!

not be put down, for your God goes forth with you. You shall not, shall not be put down!

410 Great Is Thy Faithfulness

Thomas O. Chisholm 'Faithfulness' William M. Runyan

VERSES

1. Great is Thy faith - ful-ness, O God my Fa - ther, There is no
2. Sum - mer and win - ter, and spring-time and har - vest, Sun, moon and
3. Par - don for sin and a peace that en - dur - eth, Thy own dear

shad - ow of turn - ing with Thee; Thou chang - est not, Thy com -
stars in their cours - es a - bove Join with all na - ture in
pres - ence to cheer and to guide; Strength for to - day and bright

pas - sions they fail not; As Thou hast been Thou for - ev - er wilt be.
man - i - fold wit - ness To Thy great faith - ful - ness, mer - cy and love.
hope for to - mor - row, Bless - ings all mine, with ten thou - sand be - side!

REFRAIN

Great is Thy faith - ful - ness! Great is Thy faith - ful - ness! Morn - ing by

morn - ing new mer - cies I see; All I have need - ed Thy

hand hath pro - vid - ed. Great is Thy faith - ful - ness, Lord, un - to me!

411 He's Able

Words and Music by
Paul E. Paino

He's a-ble, He's a-ble, I know He is a-ble, I know my Lord is a-ble to car-ry me through.— He's — He — heals the bro-ken heart-ed, and He sets the cap-tives free. He helps the lame to walk a-gain, and He makes the blind to see. He's

412 His Name Is Wonderful

by Audrey Mieir

His Name Is Won-der-ful, — His Name Is Won-der ful, His Name Is

Won-der-ful, Je-sus my Lord.___ He is the might-y King,___

Mas-ter of eve-ry-thing, His Name is Won-der-ful, Je-sus my Lord.

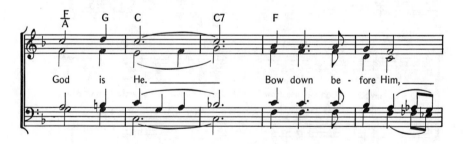

He's the Great Shep-herd, the Rock of all A - ges, Al - might-y

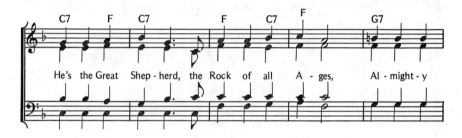

God is He.___ Bow down be-fore Him,___

Love and a - dore Him. His Name is Won-der-ful, Je-sus my Lord.

413   How Great Thou Art

by Stuart K. Hine

VERSES
Capo 1, Play A

1. O Lord my God! When I in awe-some won-der Con-sid-er
2. When through the woods and for-est glades I wan-der And hear the
3. And when I think that God, His Son not spar-ing, Sent Him to
4. When Christ shall come with shout of ac-cla-ma-tion And take me

all the*worlds Thy hands have made, __ I see the stars, I hear the*roll-ing
birds sing sweet-ly in the trees; __ When I look down from loft-y moun-tain
die I scarce can take it in; __ That on the cross, my bur-den glad-ly
home, what joy shall fill my heart! __ Then I shall bow in hum-ble ad-o-

thun-der, Thy pow'r through-out the u-ni-verse dis-played, __
gran-deur And hear the brook and feel the gen-tle breeze; __ Then sings my
bear-ing, He bled and died to take a-way my sin; __
ra-tion And there pro-claim, my God, how great Thou art! __

REFRAIN

soul, my Sav-ior God to Thee; How great Thou art, how great Thou art! Then sings my

soul, my Sav-ior God to Thee; How great Thou art, how great Thou art!

414   Let the Righteous Be Glad

Psalm 68 adapted by
Mark B. Foster

Music by
Mark B. Foster

Capo 3, Play Bm

1. Let God a-rise, let his en-e-mies be scat-tered; let those who hate him flee be-fore him! As smoke is driv-en, so drive them a-way; As wax melts be-fore the fire.

REFRAIN

Let the right-eous be glad, ex-ult-ing be-fore God ju-bi-lant with joy! Sing to God, sing prais-es to his name lift up a song to him who rides up-on the clouds. clouds. Let the clouds. Lift up a song to him who rides up-on the clouds.

VERSES

2. O God when you went forth be-fore your peo-ple, when you marched through the wil-der-ness, the earth quaked, the heav-ens poured down rain at the pres-ence of the God of Is-ra-el. Let the

3. With might-y char-iots, thou-sands up-on thou-sands, the Lord came to the ho-ly— place.

You as-cend-ed lead-ing cap-tives in your train, And re - ceiv - ing gifts a- mong—men. Let the

4. Sum-mon your might, O God, show forth your strength, you who have con-quered for us.

Our God is a God of sal-va-tion; to him be-longs es - cape— from death. Let the

5. He sends forth his voice, his might-y voice, he who rides in the an - cient

heav-ens— Sing to God, O king-doms of the earth; sing prais-es to— the Lord. Let the

6. Awe-some is the Lord in his sanc-tu - a - ry, whose maj-es-ty is o-ver— Is - ra-el.

He gives pow-er and strength to his peo-ple; bless-ed be— our God! Let the

415 Lift Up Your Heads, O Gates

C9

Psalm 24 adapted by
Martha Ilgenfritz

Music by
Martha Ilgenfritz

REFRAIN

up, lift up your heads, O— gates, And be

lift - ed up, O an - cient doors, _____ Lift

up, lift up your heads, O— gates, That the

King of Glo - ry may _ come in. _____ 1. The in. _____ Lift

VERSES

(1.) earth is the Lord's and the ful - ness there - of, The

world and those who dwell there - in, _____ For

he has found - ed it up - on the__ seas And es -

416 The Lord Is My Shepherd

Psalm 23

Music by
Donald E. Fishel

The Lord is my shep-herd; there is noth-ing I shall want. The want. 1. The want. 2. He 3. You 4. On-ly

(1.) LORD is my shep-herd; I shall not want. In ver-dant pas-tures he gives me re-pose; Be-side rest-ful wa-ters he

417 The Lord Reigns

Psalm 97 adapted by
Ted Kennedy III

Music by
Ted Kennedy III

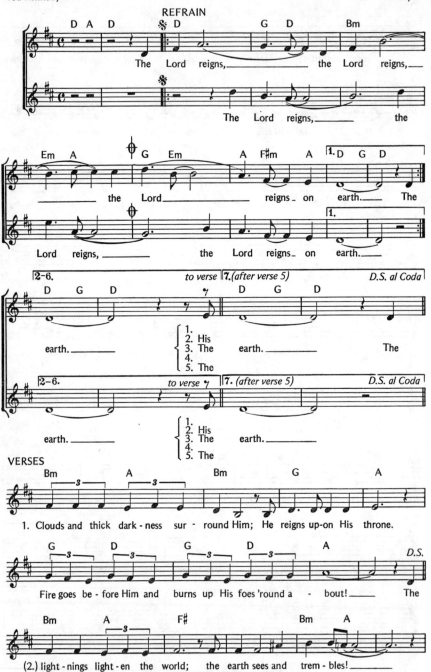

418 Mighty Is Our God

Words and Music by
Steve Alaniz

O For a Thousand Tongues to Sing 419

'Azmon'

Charles Wesley, 1707-1778

Carl G. Glaser, 1784-1829
Arr. Lowell Mason, 1792-1872

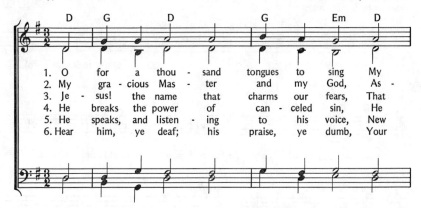

1. O for a thou - sand tongues to sing My
2. My gra - cious Mas - ter and my God, As -
3. Je - sus! the name that charms our fears, That
4. He breaks the power of can - celed sin, He
5. He speaks, and listen - ing to his voice, New
6. Hear him, ye deaf; his praise, ye dumb, Your

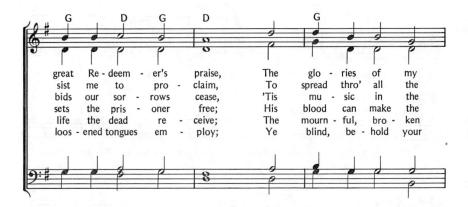

great Re - deem - er's praise, The glo - ries of my
sist me to pro - claim, To spread thro' all the
bids our sor - rows cease, 'Tis mu - sic in the
sets the pris - oner free; His blood can make the
life the dead re - ceive; The mourn - ful, bro - ken
loos - ened tongues em - ploy; Ye blind, be - hold your

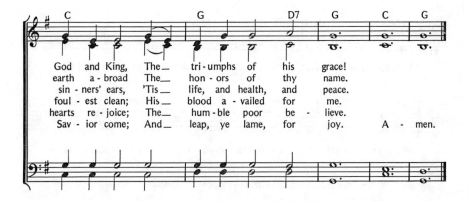

God and King, The tri - umphs of his grace!
earth a - broad The hon - ors of thy name.
sin - ners' ears, 'Tis life, and health, and peace.
foul - est clean; His blood a - vailed for me.
hearts re - joice; The hum - ble poor be - lieve.
Sav - ior come; And leap, ye lame, for joy. A - men.

420 O, Let the Redeemed

Words from Psalm 107
Adapted by Gerald Custer

Music by
Gerald Custer

2. Some were sick through their sin-ful ways, and so suf-fered af - flic - tion,__

and they drew near, near to the gates__ of death.__

Then they cried to the Lord in their trou-ble, and He de-liv-ered them from their dis-tress; He

sent forth His word and saved them from death and de - struc- tion.__

D.S.

3. Some went down to the sea in ships, do-ing busi-ness on the great wa- ters,__ but their

cour - age melt-ed a - way in their e - vil plight.__

Then they cried to the Lord in their trou-ble, and He de-liv-ered them from their dis-tress; He

made the storm__ be still, and the waves__were hushed.__

D.S.

421 Praise the Lord, O My Soul

Music by
Donald E. Fishel

Psalm 146

422 Put On Jesus Christ

Adapted from Romans 13:11-14 by
George Misulia

Music by
George Misulia

Rise Up, O Men of God

'Festal Song'

William Pierson Merrill

William H. Walter

Rise up, O men of God! Have done_with less - er things. Give
Rise up, O men of God! His King - dom tar - ries long: Bring
Rise up, O men of God! The Church_for you doth wait: Her
Lift high the cross of Christ! Tread where_ His feet have trod. As

heart, and_ soul, and mind, and strength To serve_ the_ King of kings.
in the_ day of broth - er - hood And end_ the_ night of wrong.
strength un - e - qual to her task; Rise up_ and_ make her great!
broth - ers_ of the Son of man, Rise up,_ O_ men of God!

424 Taste and See

Adapted from Psalm 34 by
George Misulia

Words and Music by
George Misulia

REFRAIN

Taste and see how good our God can be,_____ O
taste and see how good our God can be. 1. I will
2. Come__
3. The__
4. O____

5. good our God can be. Oh__ good our God can be._____

VERSES

(1.) bless the Lord at all times; my mouth will pro-claim His__ praise, my
soul makes its boast in the Lord, our God. Let the hum-ble hear and be glad. *D.S.*

(2.) glo-ri-fy the Lord with_ me, to-geth-er let us praise his_ name. Look to
him and grow bright in his ra-di-ant light and your face will nev-er be a-shamed. *D.S.*

(3.) eyes of the Lord are on the just, and his ear toward all their_ cries. The

| C | D | | G | Em | Em7 | C | Em7 | Am | Am7 | D |

Lord is near to the bro-ken heart and the crushed in spir-it he— saves. *D.S.*

| C | D | | G | G7 | C | | D | | G | G7 |

(4.) taste and see the Lord is good, and hap-py are all who trust in him. O

| C | D | | G | Em | Em7 | C | Em7 | Am | Am7 | D |

fear the Lord, you his ho-ly ones, trust in him and lack no good thing. *D.S.*

425
Thou Dost Keep Him
in Perfect Peace

Isaiah 26:3,4 adapted by
Gerald Custer

Music by
Gerald Custer

Copo 3, play D

Thou dost keep him in per - fect peace,___ whose___ mind is stayed___ on Thee;___ whose___ mind is stayed on Thee, be - cause he trusts in Thee.___ Trust in the Lord for - ev - er,___ for He is an ev - er-last - ing rock:___ Thou dost keep him in per - fect peace, whose mind___ is stayed on___ Thee. Thee.___

Thy Loving Kindness

426

Psalm 63:3-4

Words and Music by
Hugh Mitchell

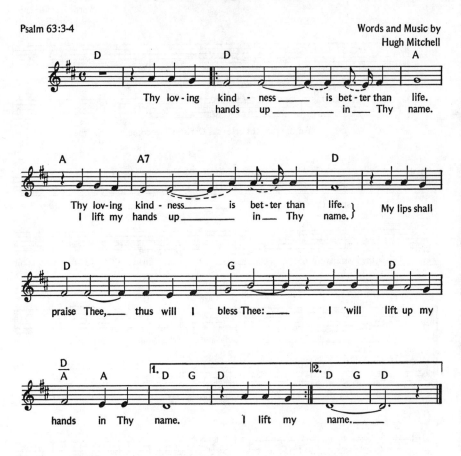

Thy lov-ing kind-ness _____ is bet-ter than life.
hands up _____ in ___ Thy name.

Thy lov-ing kind-ness _____ is bet-ter than life. } My lips shall
I lift my hands up _____ in ___ Thy name. }

praise Thee, ___ thus will I bless Thee: _____ I 'will lift up my

hands in Thy name. 1. I lift my name. 2. name. _____

427 We Are Men of Jesus Christ

Words and Music by
James Berlucchi

This song is meant to be sung in two parts by men only. On the rare occasion that it is sung in a mixed group, women may sing the descant on the refrain and join in on the third verse.

428 You Are Holy

Words adapted from Rev. 4:8,11
by Donald E. Fishel

Music by
Donald E. Fishel

CUMULATIVE INDEX

The songs numbered 1 through 79 are in *Songs of Praise, Vol. 1*; numbers 201 through 241 are in *Songs of Praise, Vol. 2;* numbers 301 through 339 are in *Songs of Praise Vol. 3;* numbers 401 through 428 are in *Songs of Praise Vol. 4.*